Lucknow and Mitchell Ontario and Area in Colour Photos, Saving Our History One Photo at a Time

Photography
by Barbara Raué
2015

Series Name:
Cruising Ontario

Book 110: Lucknow, Mitchell

Cover photo: 578 Havelock Street,
Lucknow Presbyterian Church

Series Name: Cruising Ontario
Saving Our History One Photo at a Time
in colour photos

Other Books by Barbara Raue

Coins of Gold

Arrows, Indians and Love

The Life and Times of Barbara
Volume 1: Inventions That Have Enhanced My Life
Volume 2: Entertainment That I Have Enjoyed
Volume 3: East Coast Trips
Volume 4: Olympics Have Always Intrigued Me
Volume 5: Wonders of the World
Volume 6: Caribbean Cruises We Have Enjoyed
Volume 7: Animals
Volume 8: Storms and Other Major Disasters in My Lifetime
Volume 9: Wars, Terrorist Attacks and Major Disasters

The Cromwell Family Book

Laura Secord Discovered

Daddy Where Are You?

Visit Barbara's website to view all of her books
http://barbararaue.ca

Lucknow

Lucknow is a community located in Bruce County, Ontario, located at the junction of Bruce Roads 1 and 86. Lucknow has a strong Scottish heritage back to the late 1800s when the Lucknow Caledonian Games were held for twenty years. The village was named after Lucknow, India where, in 1857, a battle Indian Rebellion of 1857 took place between the native rebels and the British army. Eli Stauffer first settled here in 1856 where he constructed a dam and built a sawmill. In 1858, Ralph Miller built Balaclava House, a log tavern.

Auburn

Auburn is located on Regional Road 24, Blyth Road on the banks of the Maitland River. The Maitland River begins in Arthur Township in Wellington County, flows west to Harriston, and continues to Howick in Huron County where it passes over two small dams, continues to Gorrie, Wroxeter, and on to Wingham where it passes over a dam and takes in the left tributary Middle Maitland River. The river turns southwest and continues through Auburn, takes in the left tributary South Maitland River, turns northwest, and goes to Goderich and reaches its mouth at Lake Huron.

Belgrave

By 1869, Belgrave was a village with a population of 50 in the Township of Morris County, Huron, on the Maitland River. It was a stop on the Buffalo and Lake Huron Railway. There were stages to Wingham, Teeswater, Riversdale and Kincardine. The average price of land was $20. Belgrave was amalgamated in 2001 by the Ontario government with Whitechurch, Blyth, and Wingham.

Carlow

Carlow/Mayo is a township in northern Hastings County and was forrmed in 2001 by the amalgamation of the townships of Carlow and Mayo. Historically, the economy in the area was based on timber and mining. The Little Mississippi River and York River were used to transport logs out of the forests. Now, tourism is an important part of the local economy. Carlow and Mayo were named after the counties of the same name in Ireland.

Dunlop

Dunlop is located on Highway 21 and County Road 25, north of Goderich.

Dublin

Dublin was founded in 1849 when U. C. Lee opened a store, on Huron Road 8. A small stream enters the village at its northern limit. Salt was discovered at Seaforth, five miles to the west, and through the enterprising efforts of Joseph Kidd, salt was brought in conduit pipes to Dublin where salt blocks were built and provided employment to a large number of workmen. Mr. Kidd also built a sawmill, and a block of brick stores on Main Street.

Mitchell

Mitchell is located at the intersection of Highways 8 and 23, east of Seaforth and 20 kilometres west of Stratford. Mitchell was founded in 1836 by William Johnston, who laid out a town plot and local tavern, and John Hicks, one of the first settlers of the area, who erected a hotel near the Thames River, where the historic Hicks House Hotel building (now restored with stores and apartments) in downtown Mitchell stands. A sawmill was built in 1842, as well as new stores and businesses, contributing to the town's growth.

Walton

Walton is located at the intersection of Huron County Road 12 and Road 25, 45 kilometres east of Goderich. Situated at the junction of Morris, Grey and McKillop Townships on the Seaforth-to-Wroxeter trail, Walton is named for the English hometown of its founders John and Anna (Button) Hewitt. Hewitt was born in Walton in Buckinghamshire, England and married Anna Button there. They sailed for Upper Canada in 1843 and settled in this area. The American Civil War (1861-1865) generated a widespread economic boom. Soon there were two stores, a lodging house, a blacksmith shop, sawmill and gristmill. Rob Roy and Walton Hotels were built and postal service began in 1862 in one of the stores. The Walton Hotel was the most successful and it still functions as an inn and restaurant today. Through the years there were pump makers, butchers, barbers, jewellers, lawyers, blacksmiths, carriage makers, harness makers, livery stable operators, doctors, veterinarians, bankers, implement dealers and garages. The Canadian Pacific Railway began running through the village in 1907 and continued operations until 1988. The first log schoolhouse was built in 1860

Whitechurch

Whitechurch is a village near Lucknow, Ontario, located along the border of Huron and Bruce County. Whitechurch is a residential community, with the Chalmers Presbyterian Church, Whitechurch Community Hall and CMG Building Solutions. The Whitechurch United Church closed on June 24, 2007.

Winthrop

Winthrop is a very small village located on the southeastern part of Huron County, where two county roads, Winthrop and Kippen (N Line), meet. Winthrop has a few shops, a general store, and a post office.

Table of Contents

Lucknow

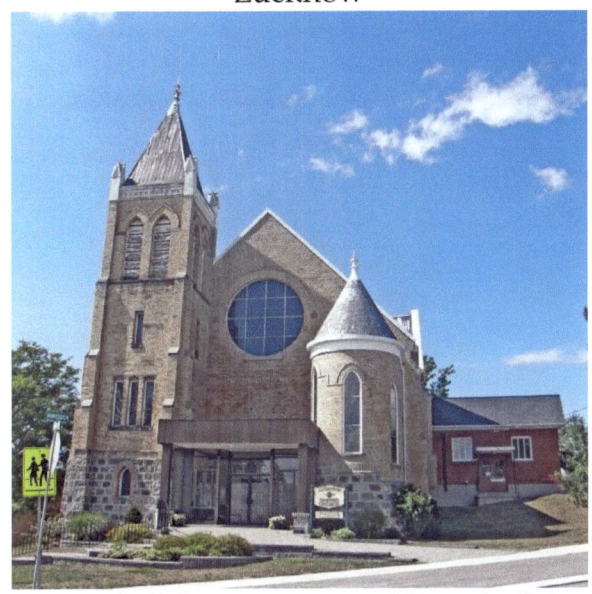

505 Campbell Street, corner of Havelock Street
Lucknow United Church – 1885 – bell tower, turret

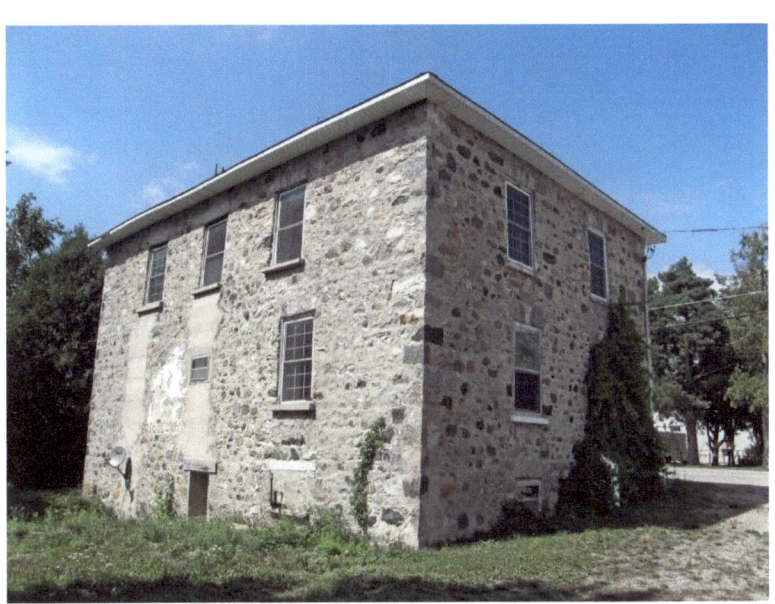

Cobblestone building

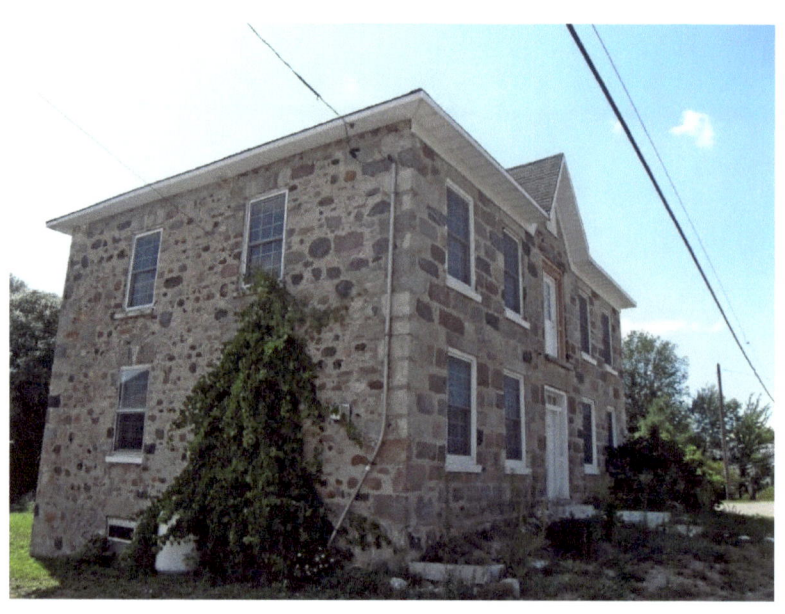

Cobblestone architecture

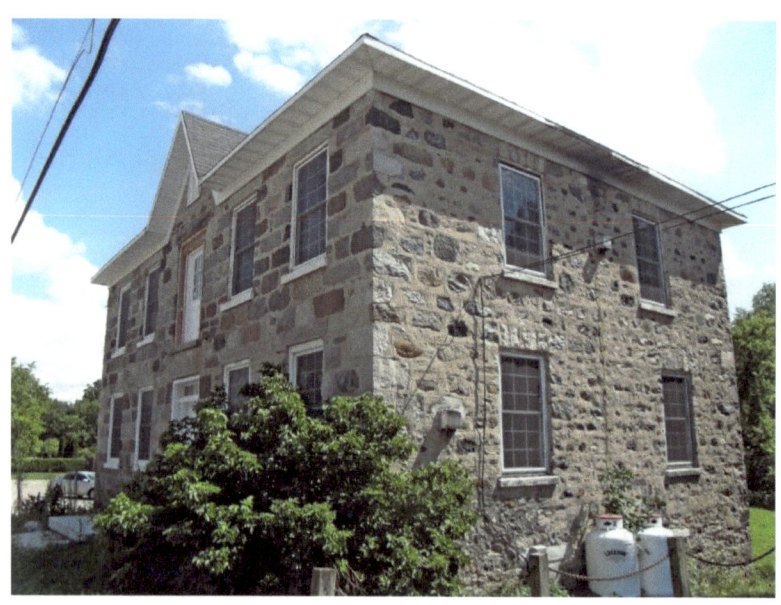

The first waterworks of Lucknow village to server for fire protections was operated from a white brick building built on the west side of the river in 1890 and served for fire protection until 1931. Water was taken from the river and a wood-fired steam boiler supplied the energy to operate a pump that pumped water through the mains. A steam whistle at the waterworks engine house alerted the firemen.

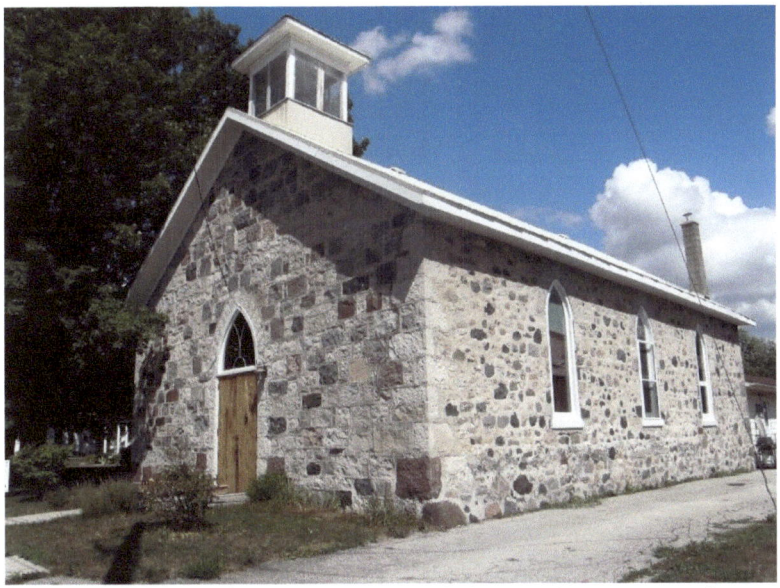

I.H.S. Church – 1873 – Church of the Holy Name of Jesus, cobblestone architecture, cupola, lancet windows

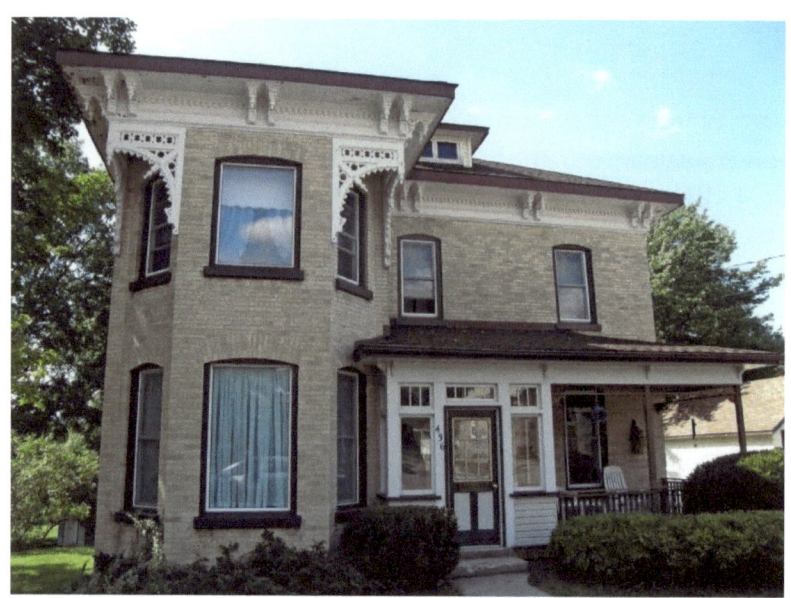

436 Campbell Street – Italianate style - paired cornice brackets, fretwork, dormer

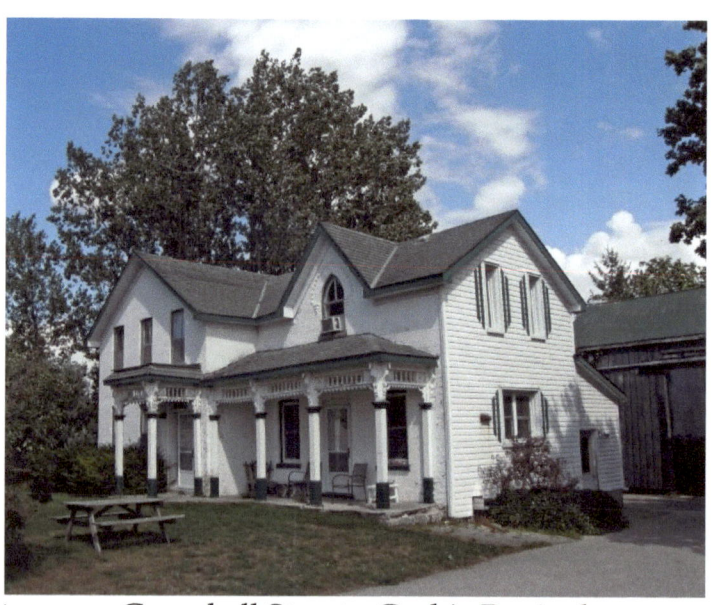

Campbell Street - Gothic Revival

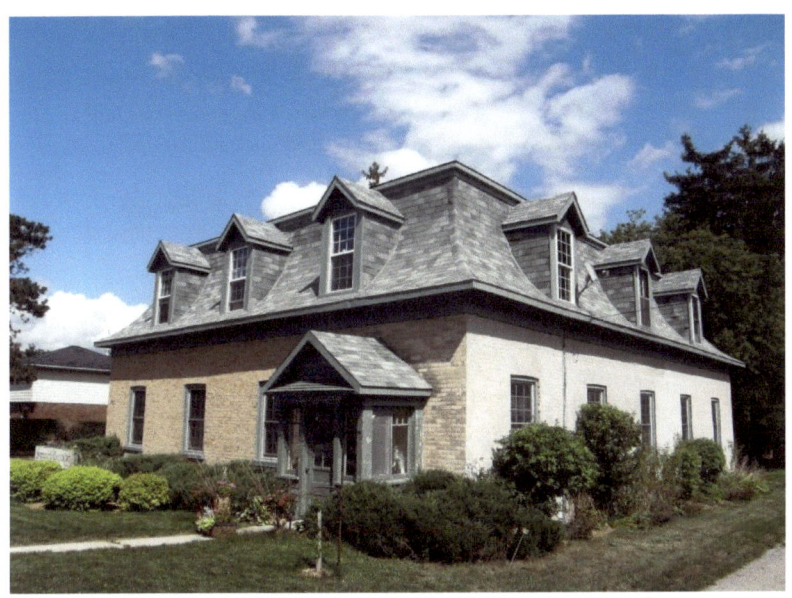

Campbell Street - Second Empire style,
mansard roof with dormers

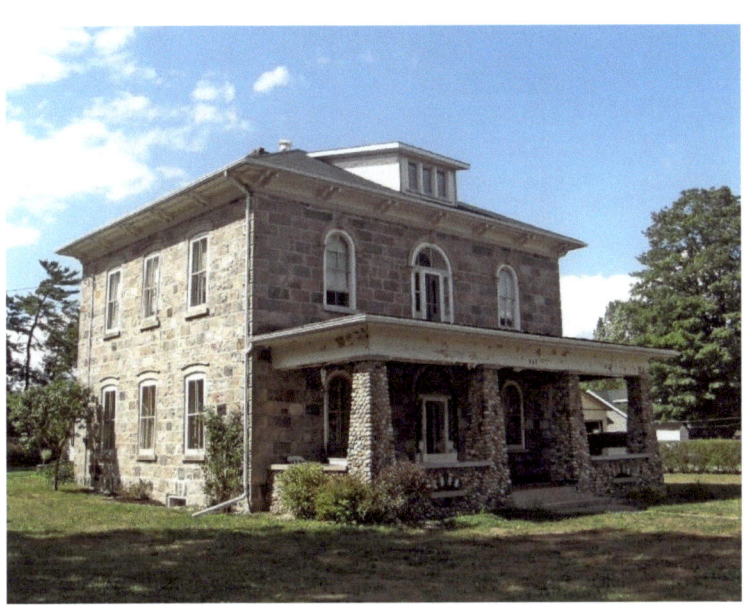

Campbell Street - Italianate, hipped roof, dormer

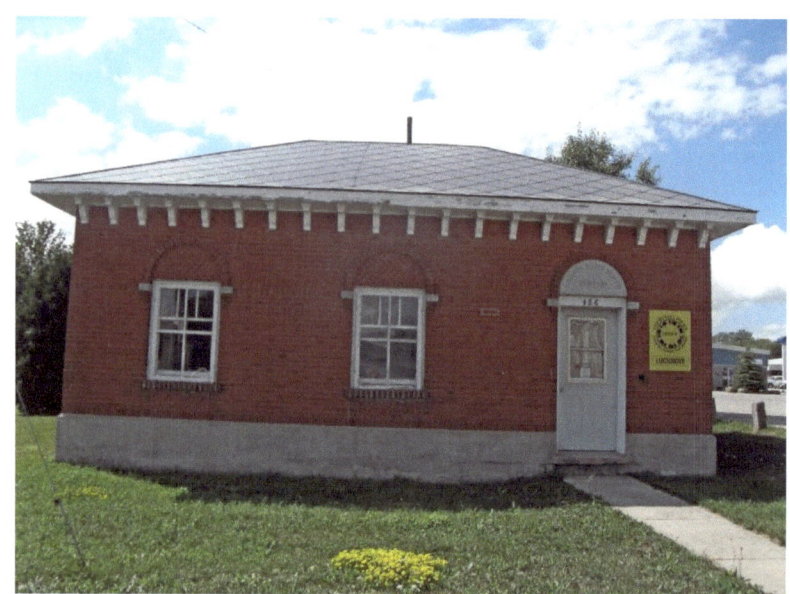

Campbell Street - Italianate, cornice brackets, hipped roof

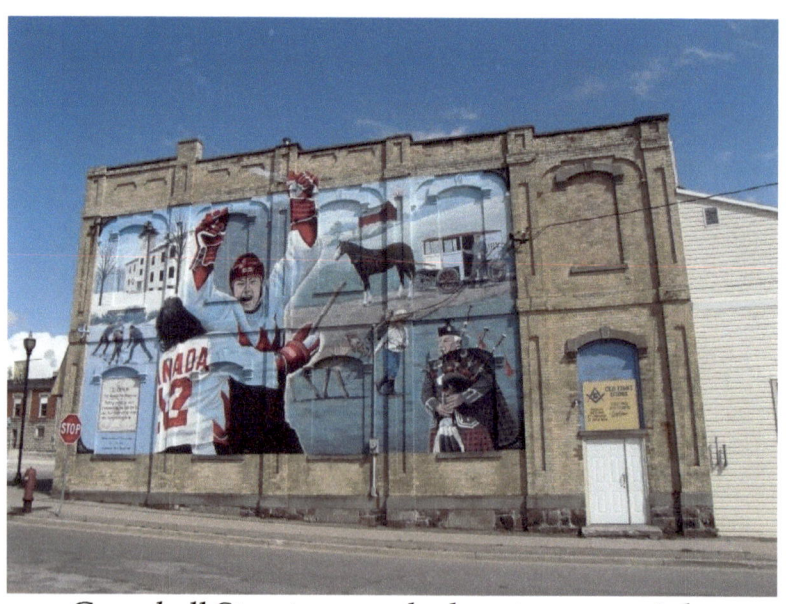

Campbell Street – mural – keystones on right

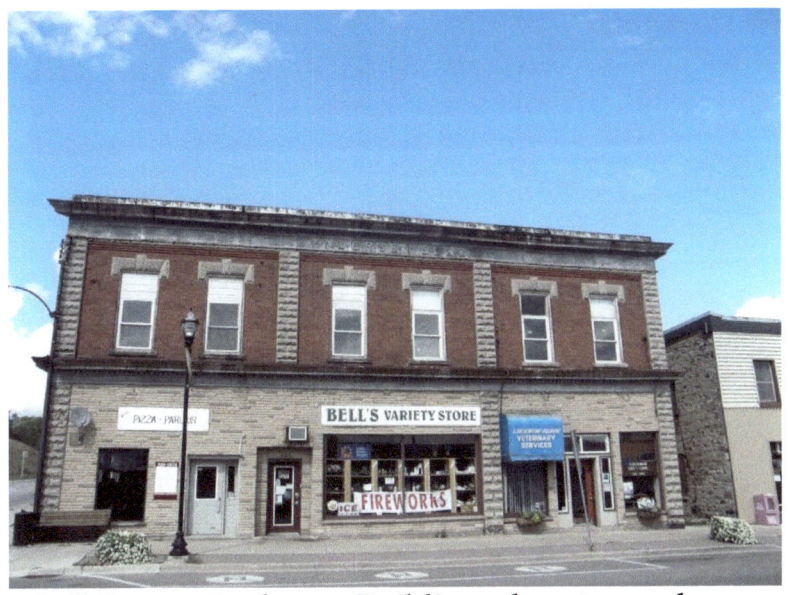

Campbell Street - Anderson Building – keystones above upper
windows, corner quoins, pilasters

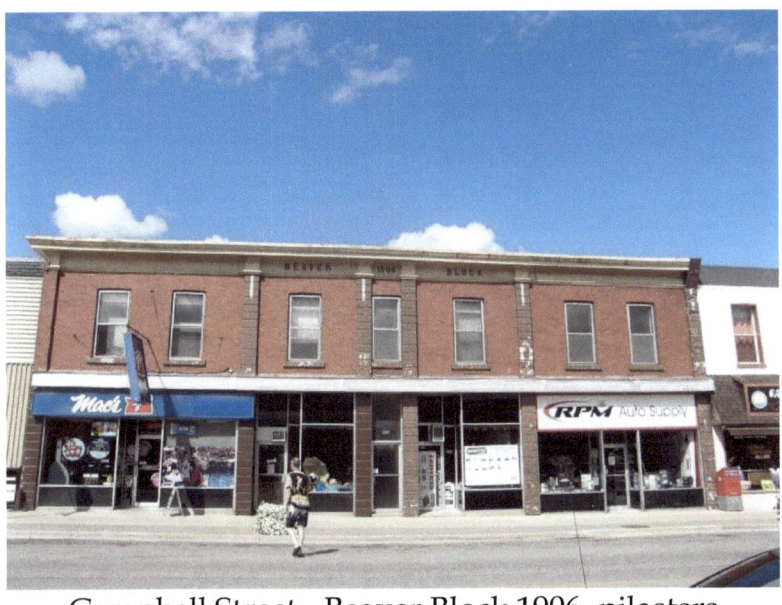

Campbell Street - Beaver Block 1906, pilasters

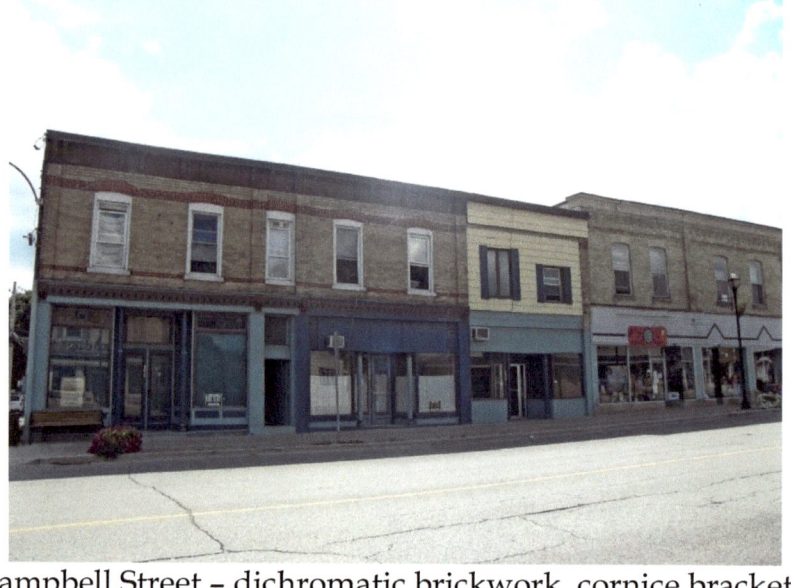

Campbell Street – dichromatic brickwork, cornice brackets, bevelled dentil moulding

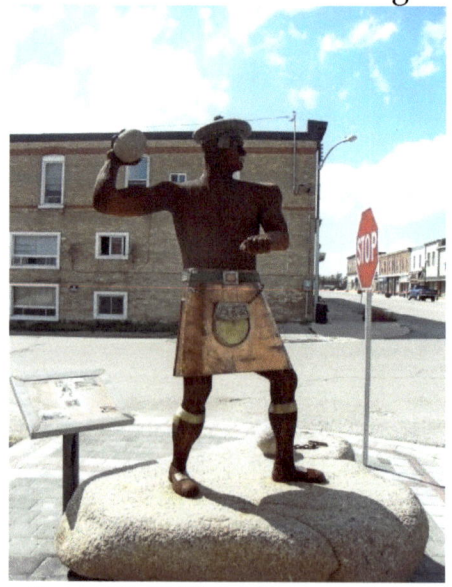

Donald Dinnie, a Scottish athlete known for his incredible strength, competed at many Caledonian Games held in Lucknow in the late 19th century.

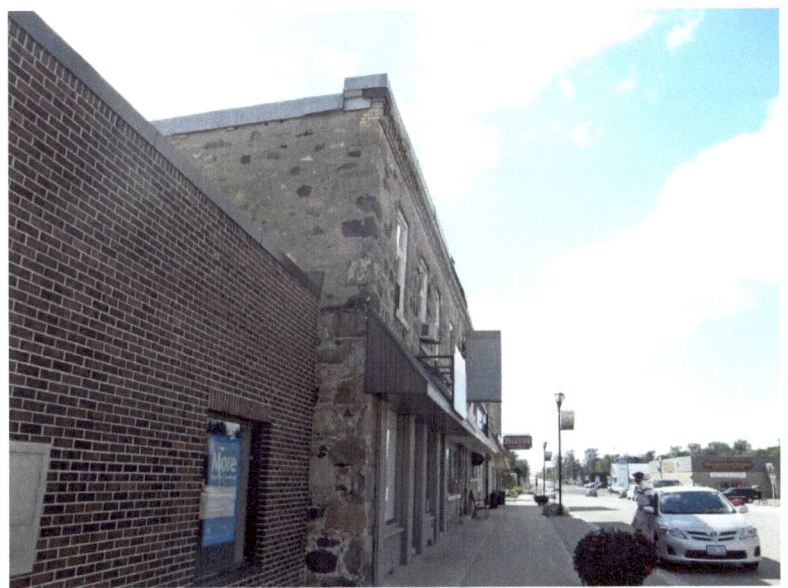

Inglis Street

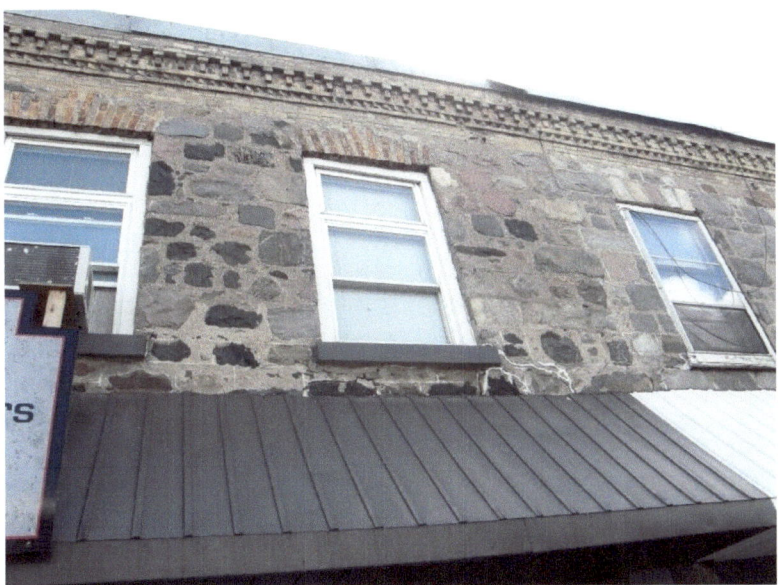

Cobblestone, dentil moulding, dichromatic voussoirs

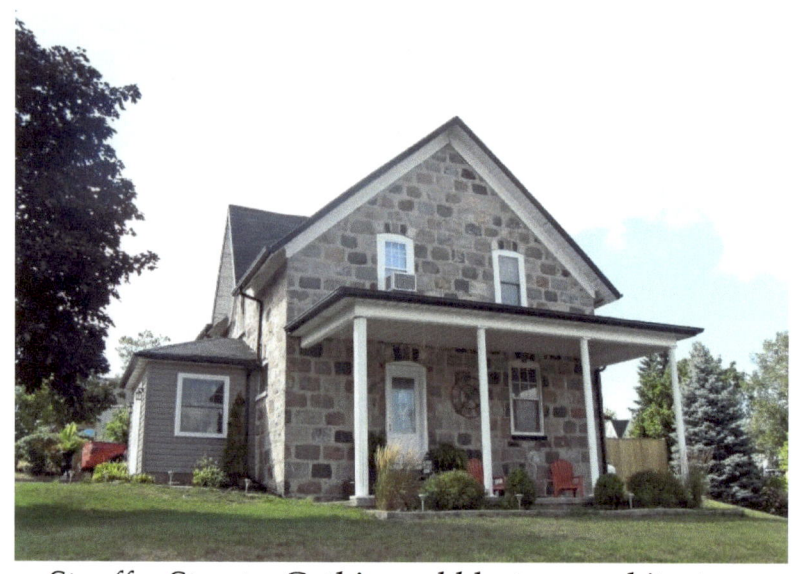

Stauffer Street – Gothic - cobblestone architecture

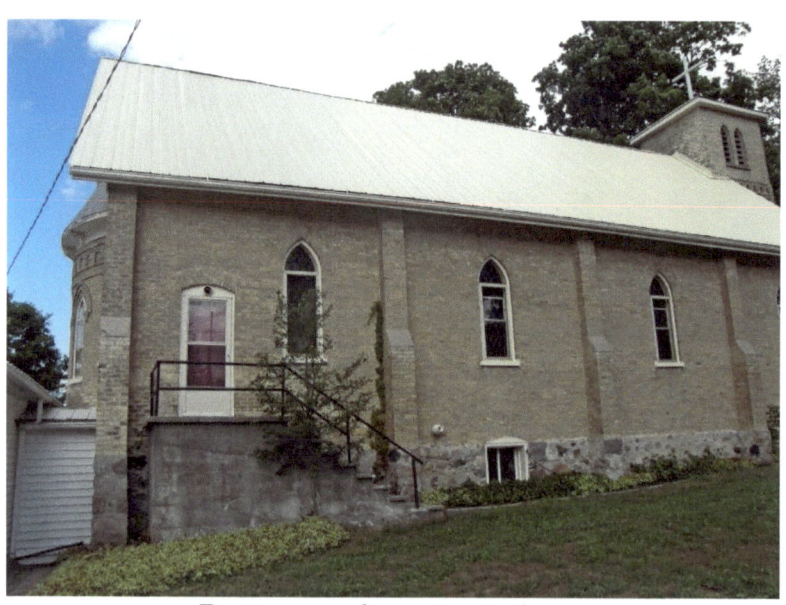

Buttresses, lancet windows

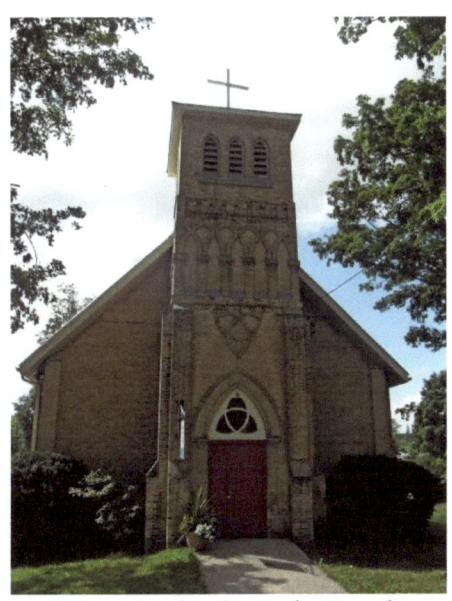

592 Outram Street - St. Peter's Anglican Church

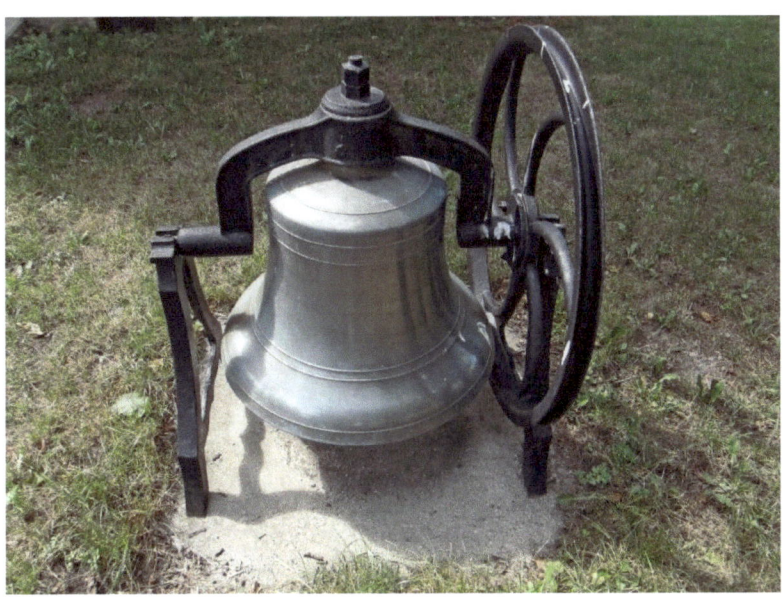

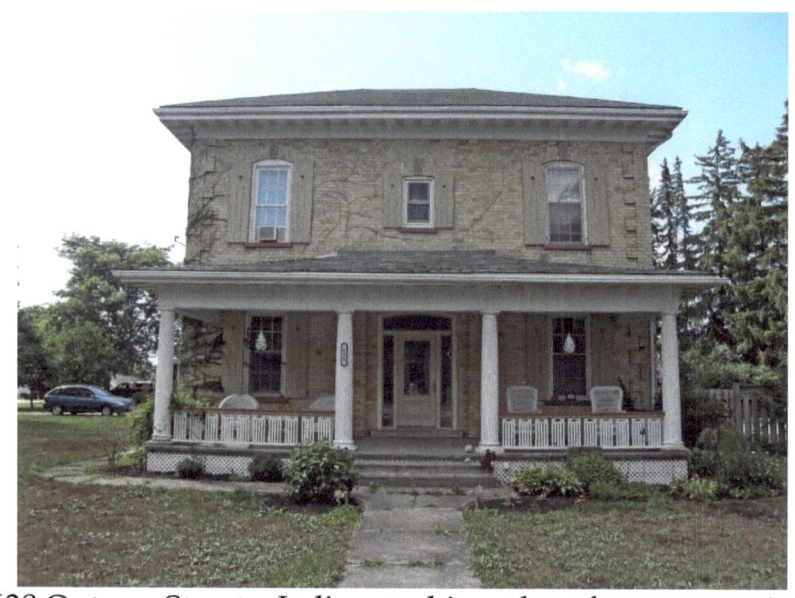

638 Outram Street – Italianate, hipped roof, corner quoins, voussoirs, keystones

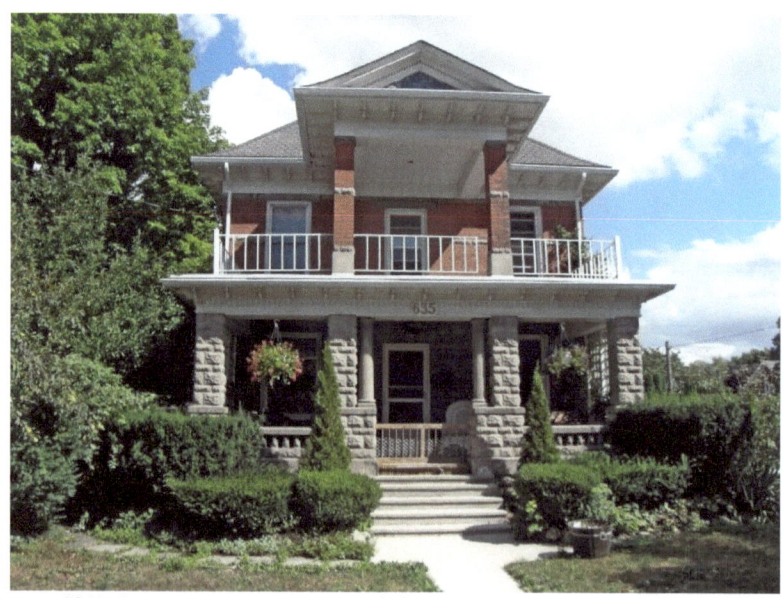

635 Outram Street – 2nd floor balcony, pediment

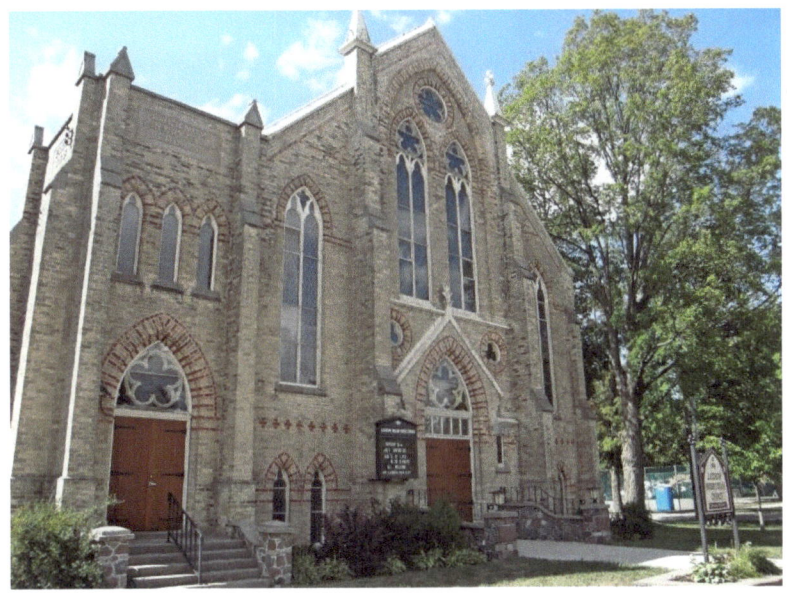

578 Havelock Street - Lucknow Presbyterian Church
erected 1889

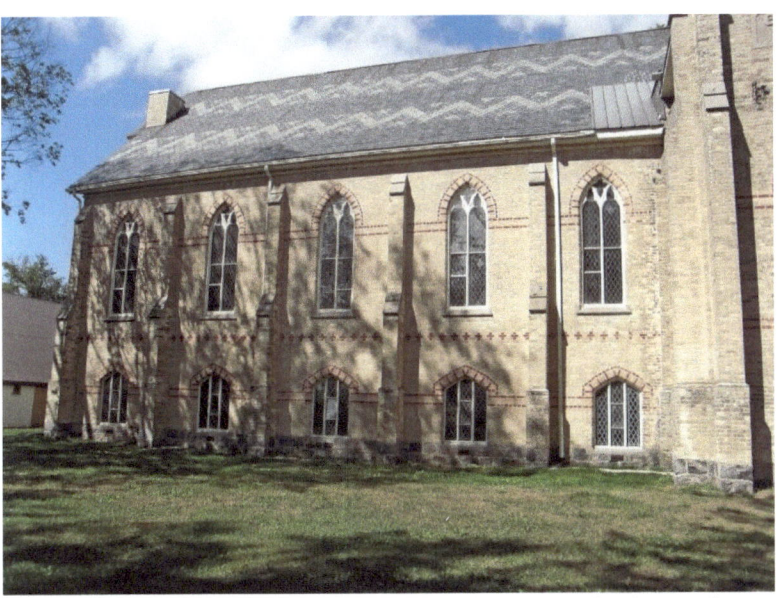

Buttresses, dichromatic brickwork and tilework

Auburn

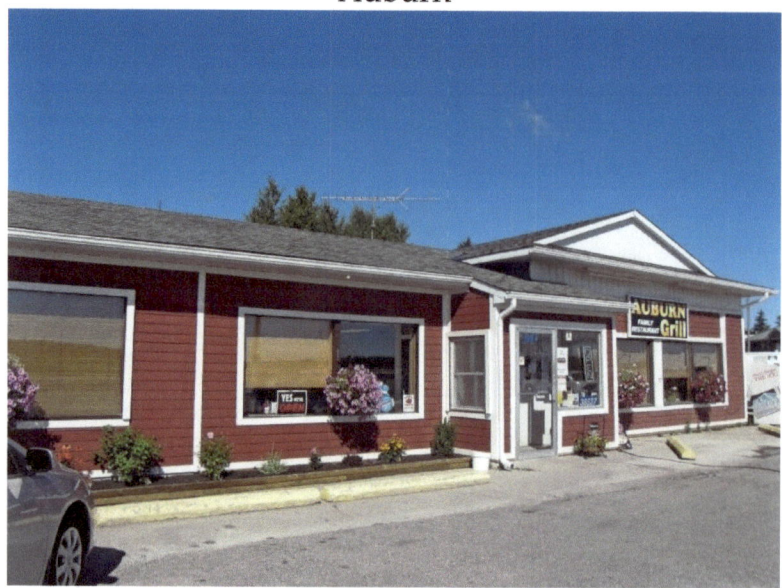

Auburn Grill Family Restaurant

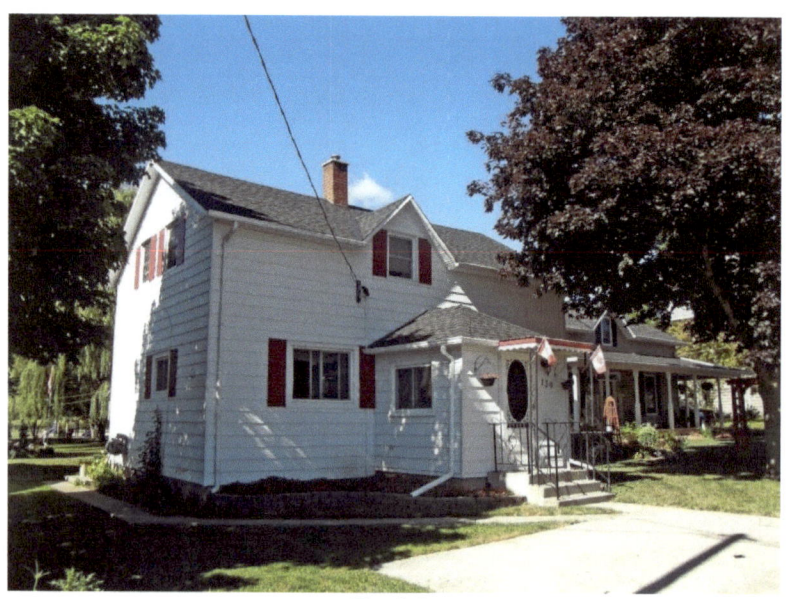

Gothic

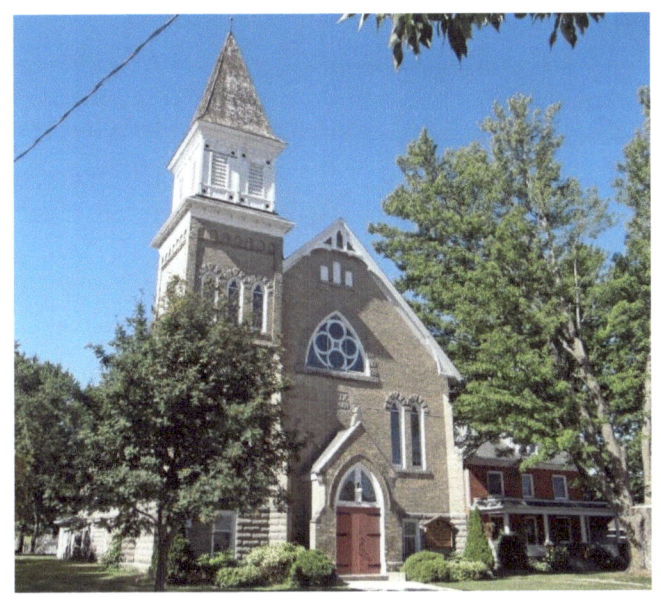

Auburn Knox United Church, rose window, lancet windows

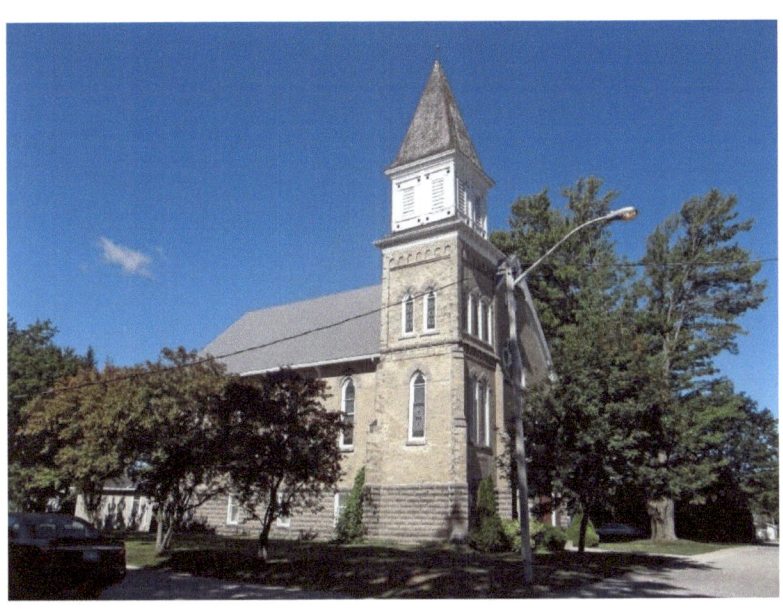

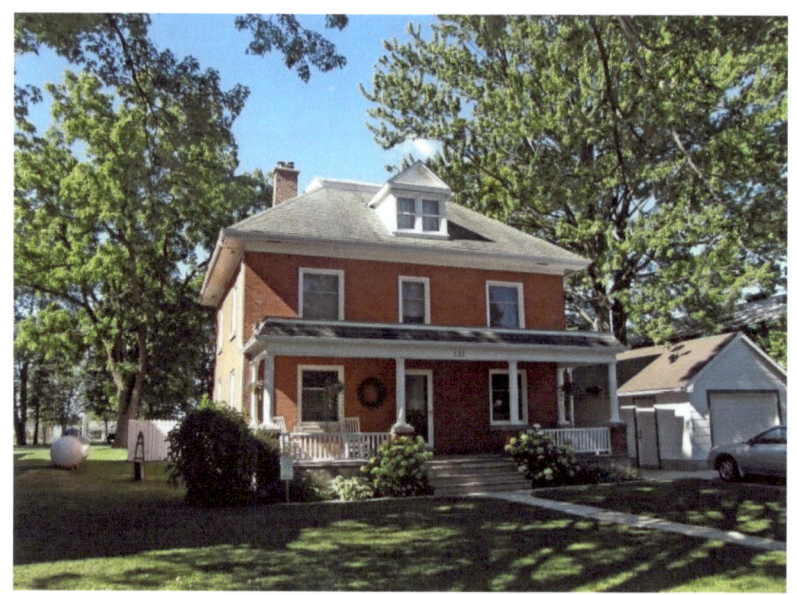

Italianate, dormer in attic

Belgrave

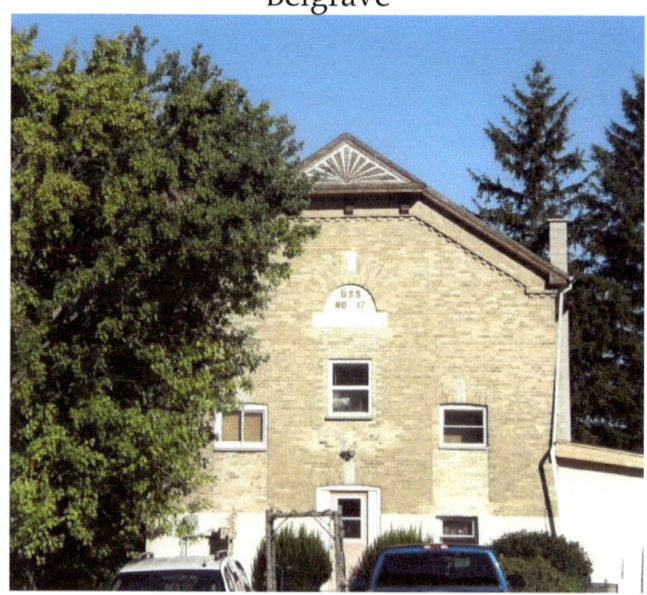

U.S.S. No. 17 - school

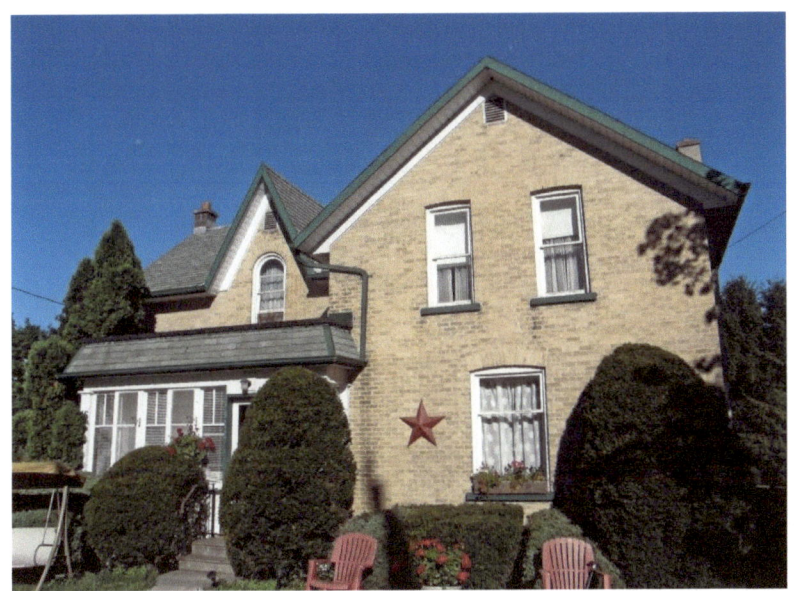

Gothic Revival

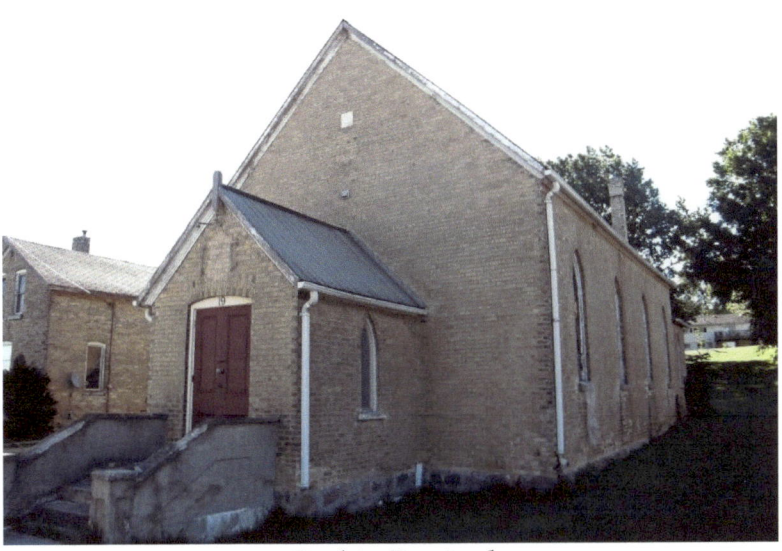

Gothic Revival

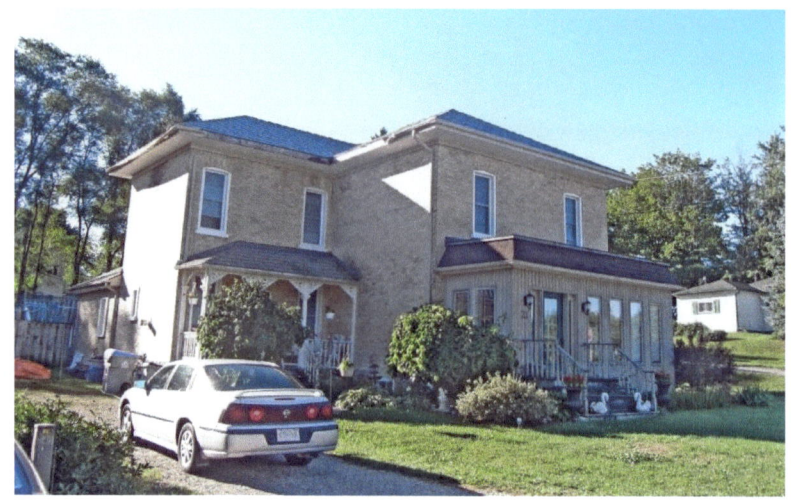

Italianate – hipped roof

Carlow

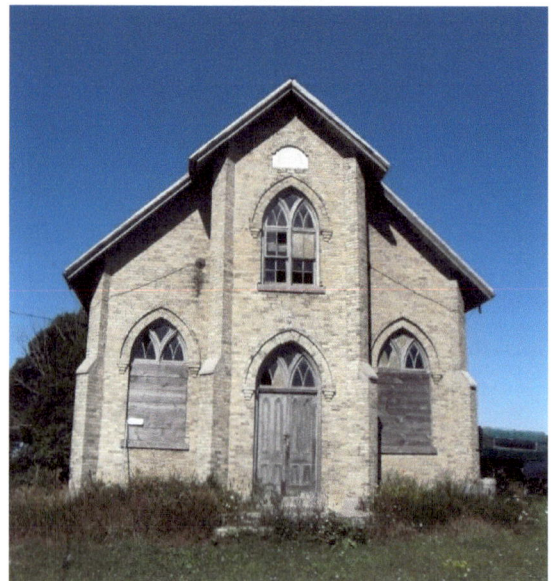

Presbyterian Church erected A.D. 1872 - buttresses

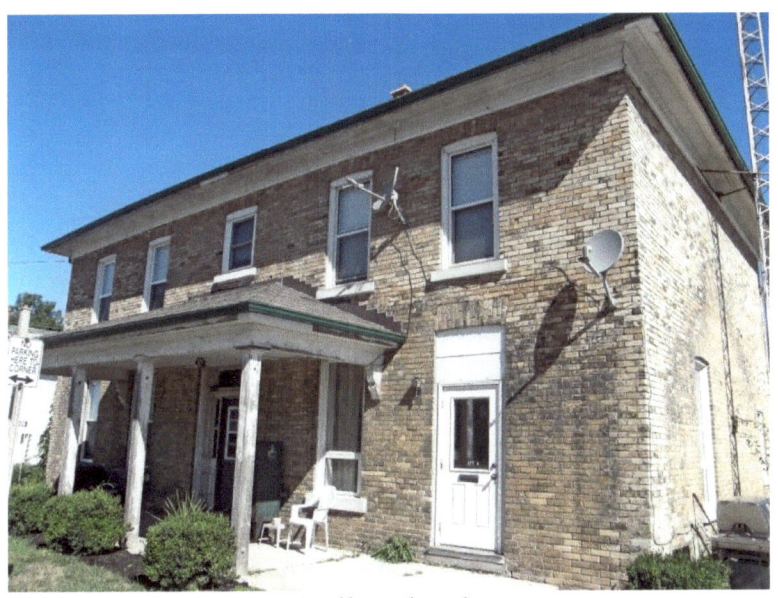

Yellow brick

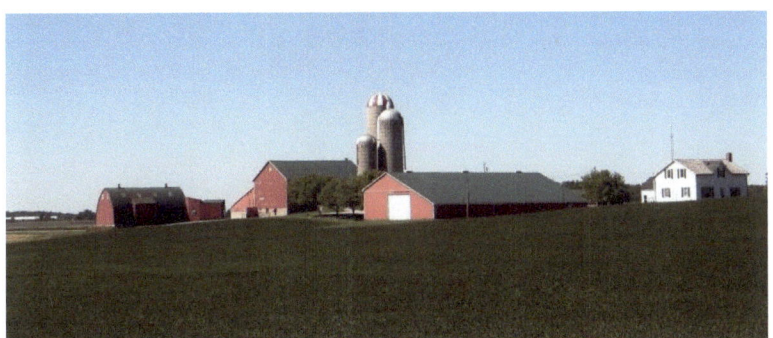

Dublin

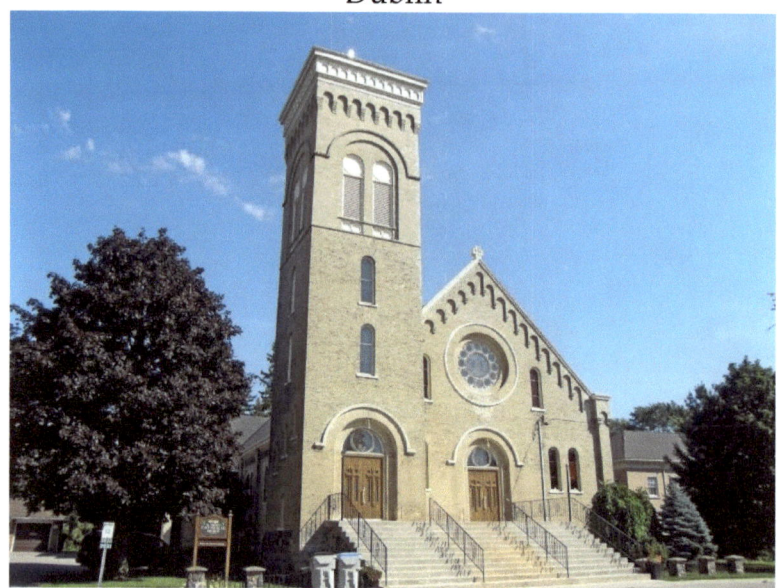

St. Patrick's Catholic Church, Dublin – rose window, dentil moulding

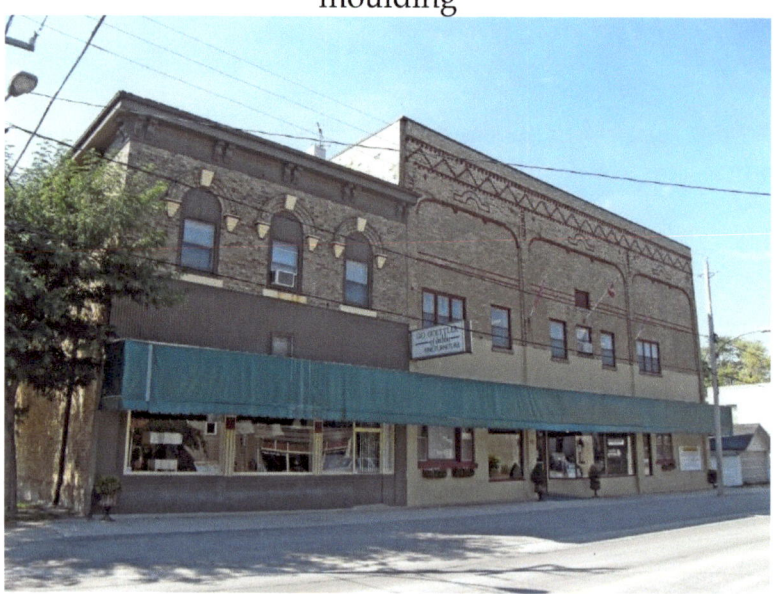

Dichromatic brickwork, voussoirs and keystones, cornice brackets

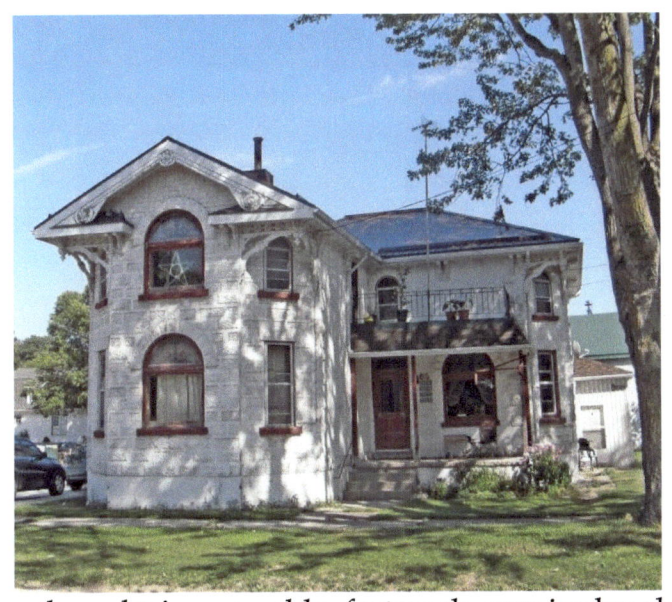

Verge board trim on gable, fretwork, cornice brackets, Romanesque style window arches

Dunlop

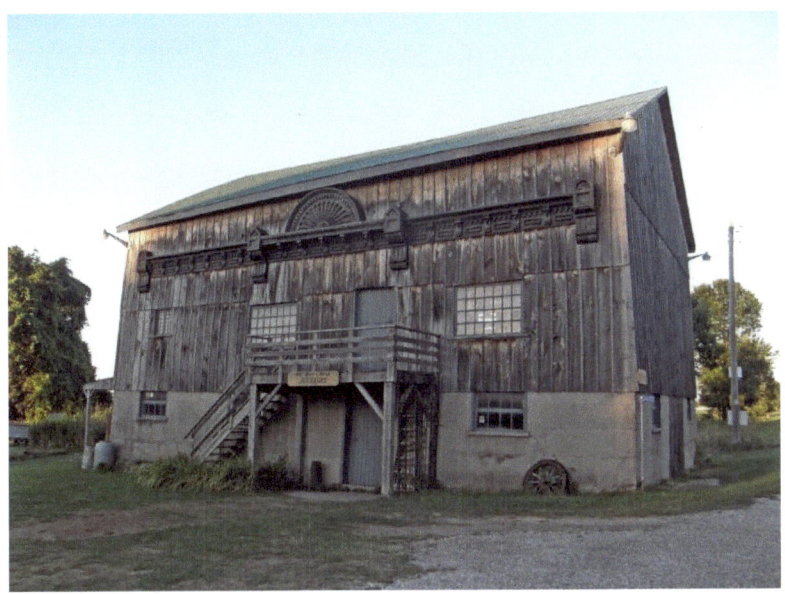

Mitchell

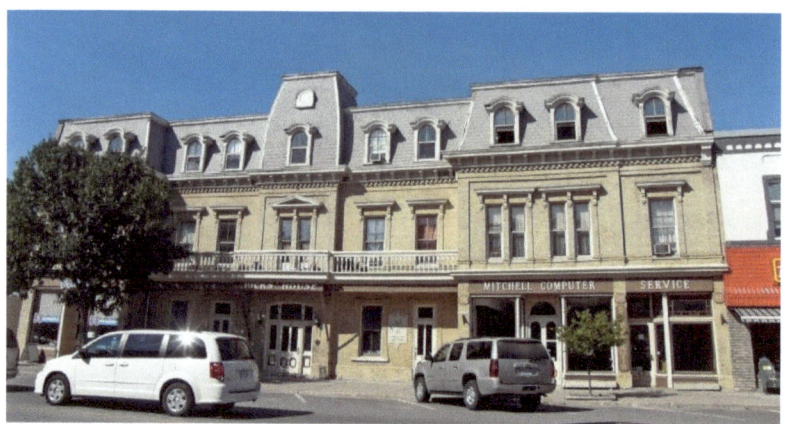

Second Empire style – mansard roof, dormers, window hoods, dentil moulding, second floor balcony

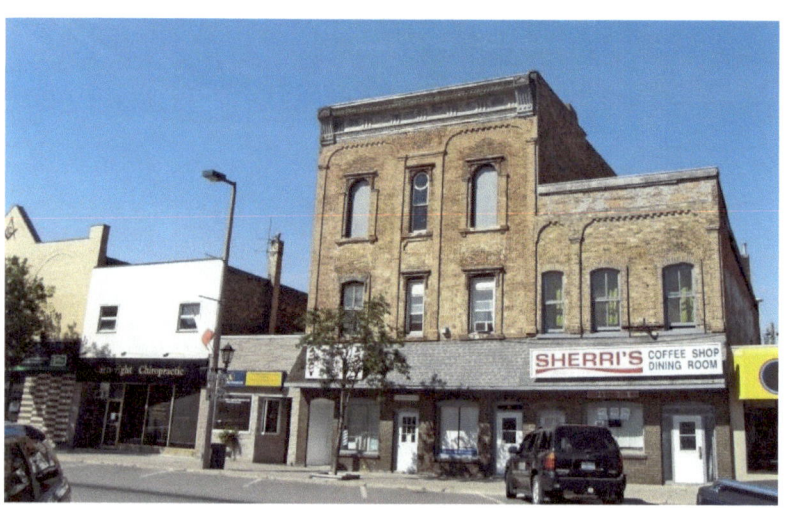

Pilasters, dentil moulding

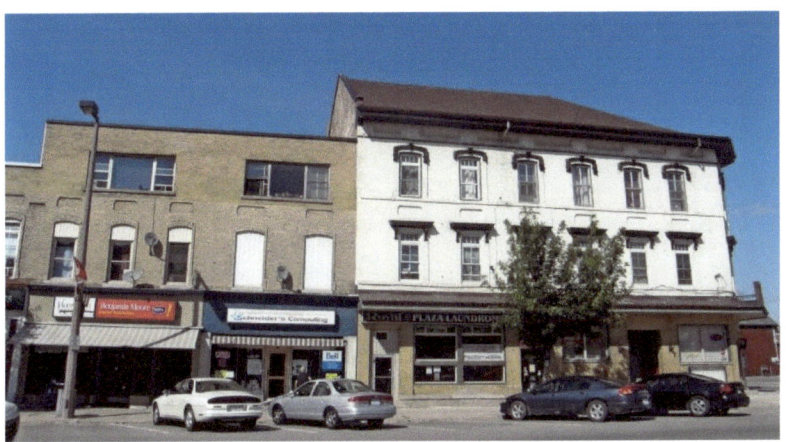

Keystones, window hoods

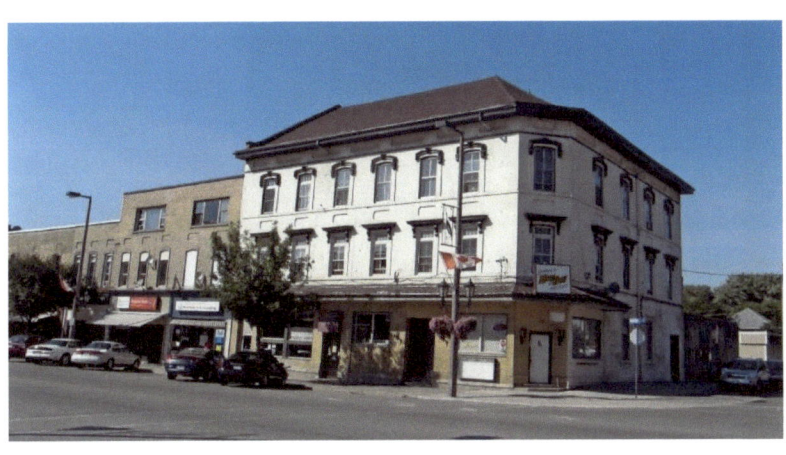

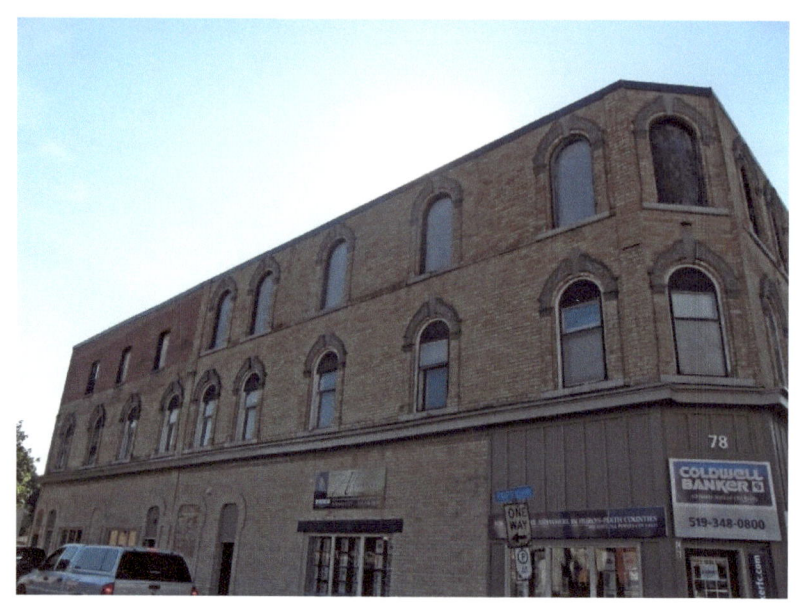

#78 - voussoirs, keystones

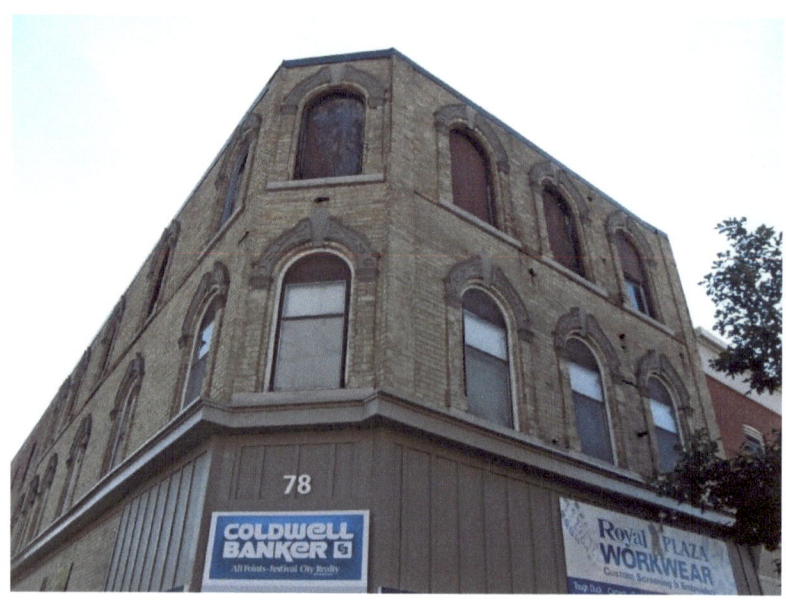

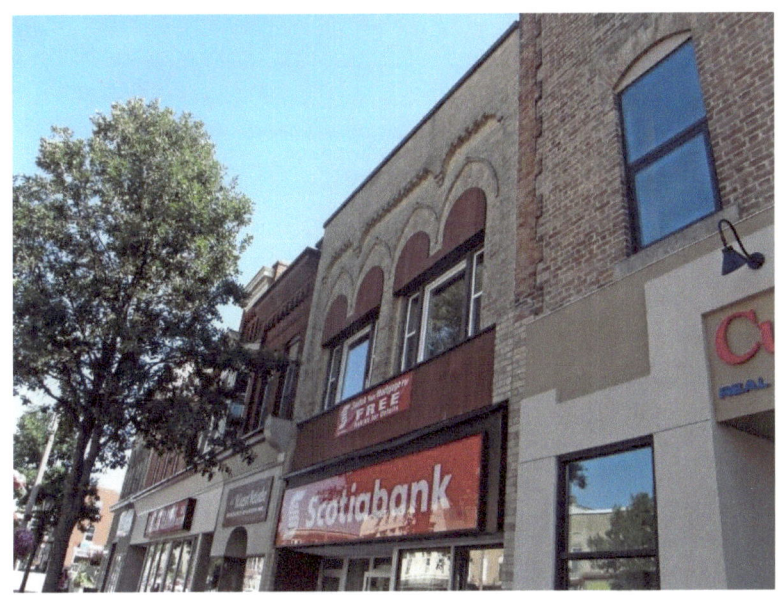

Dentil moulding

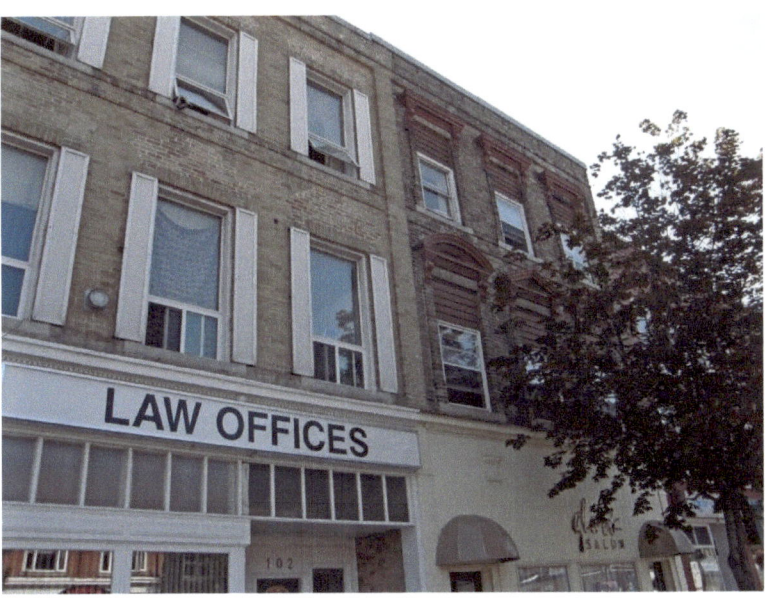

Window hoods

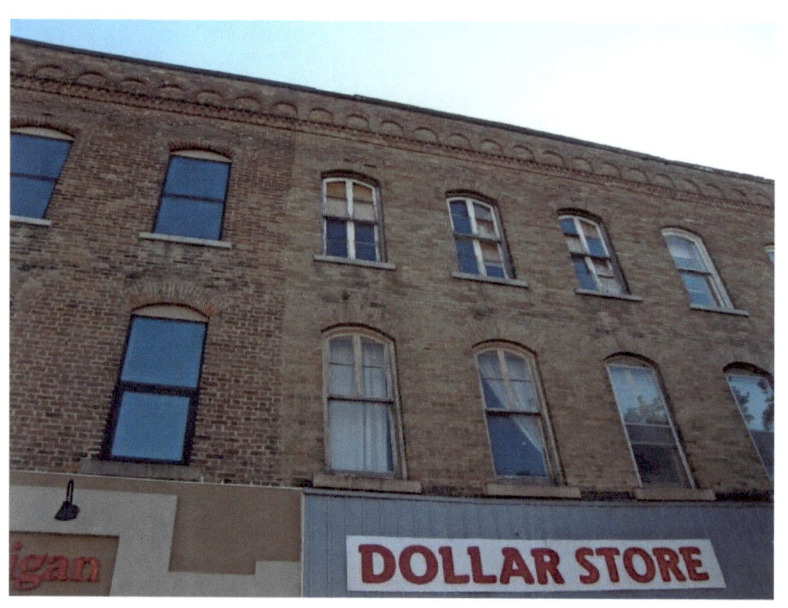

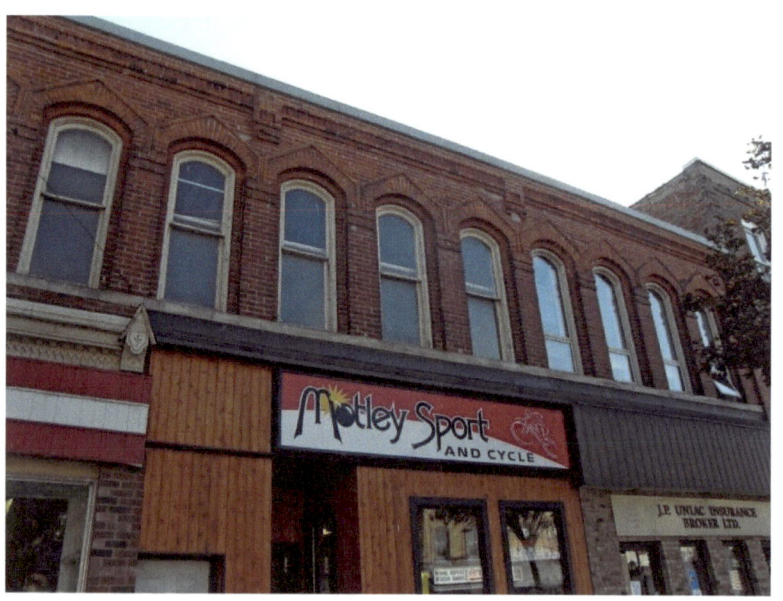

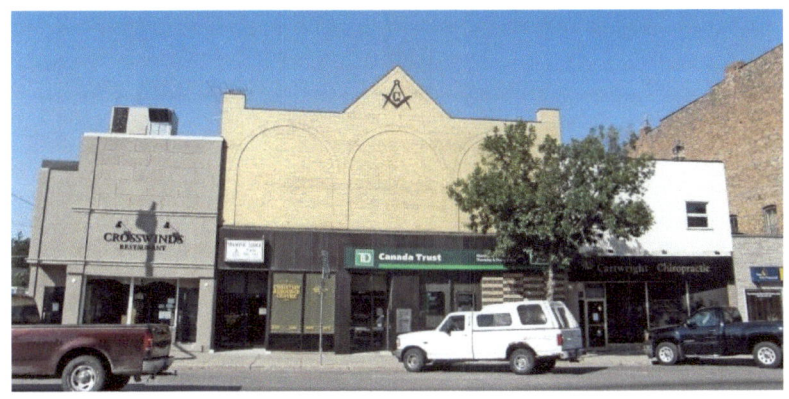

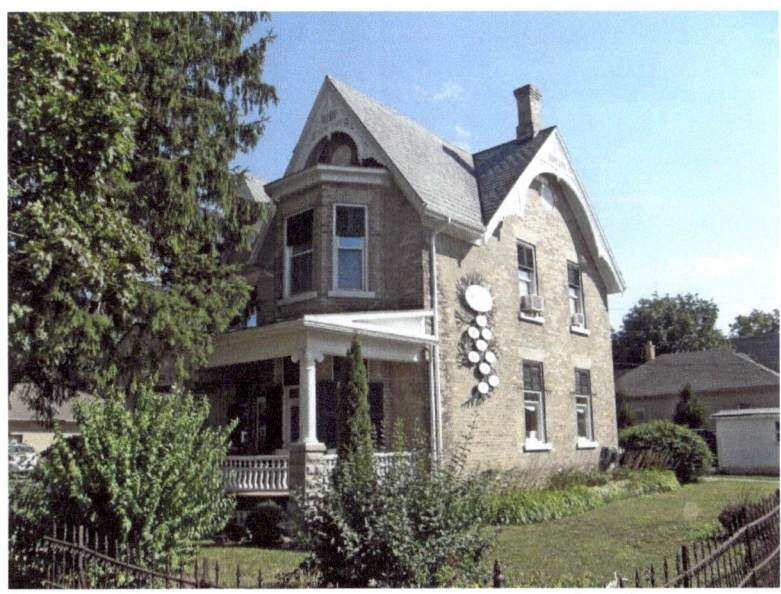

Gothic Revival – verge board trim on gables, bay window

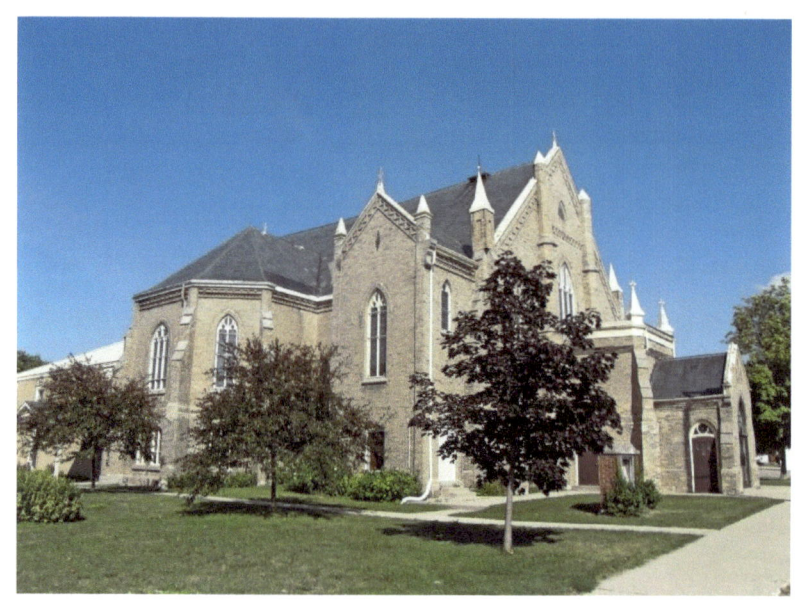

Main Street United Church 1886

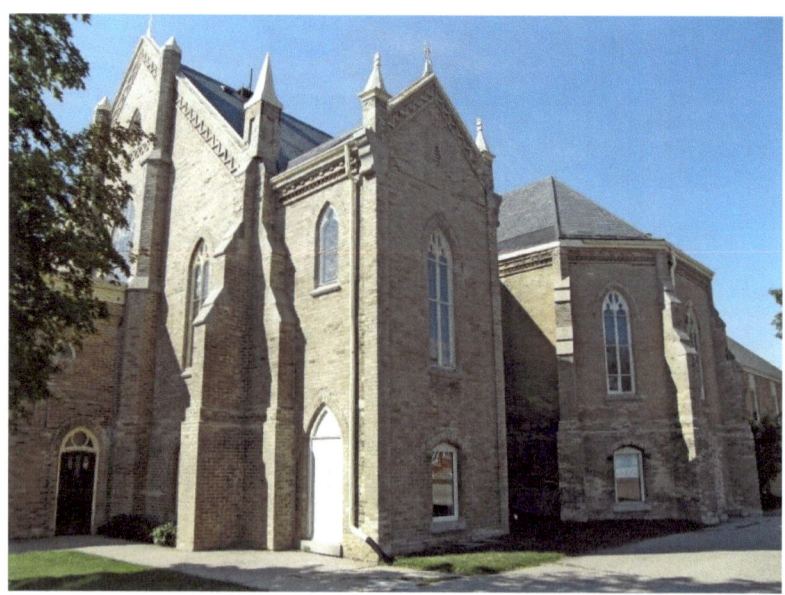

Buttresses with finials, lancet windows

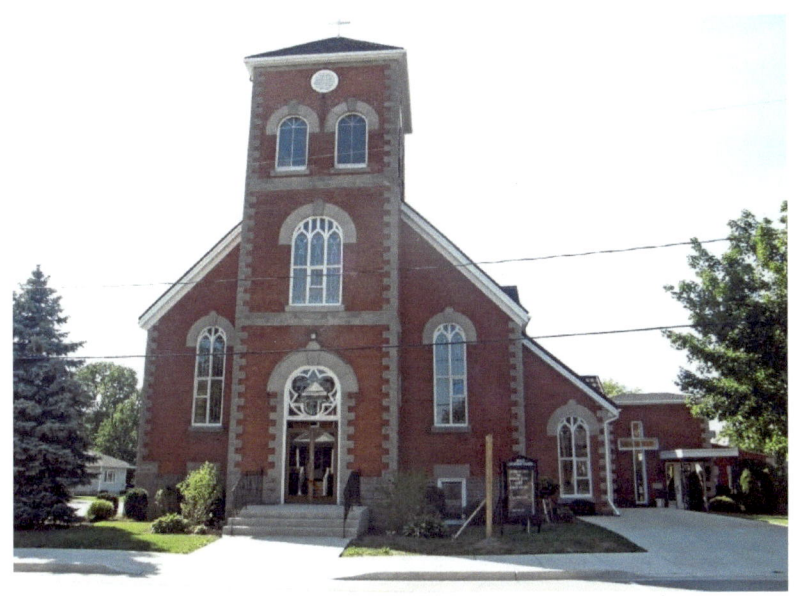

Grace Lutheran Church – erected A.D. 1913, corner quoins

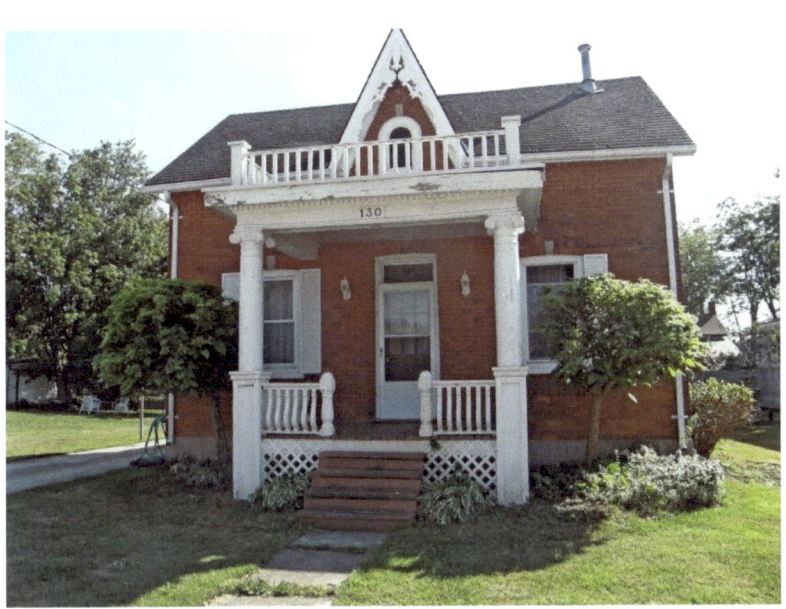

#130 – Gothic Revival, 2nd floor balcony,
verge board trim on gable

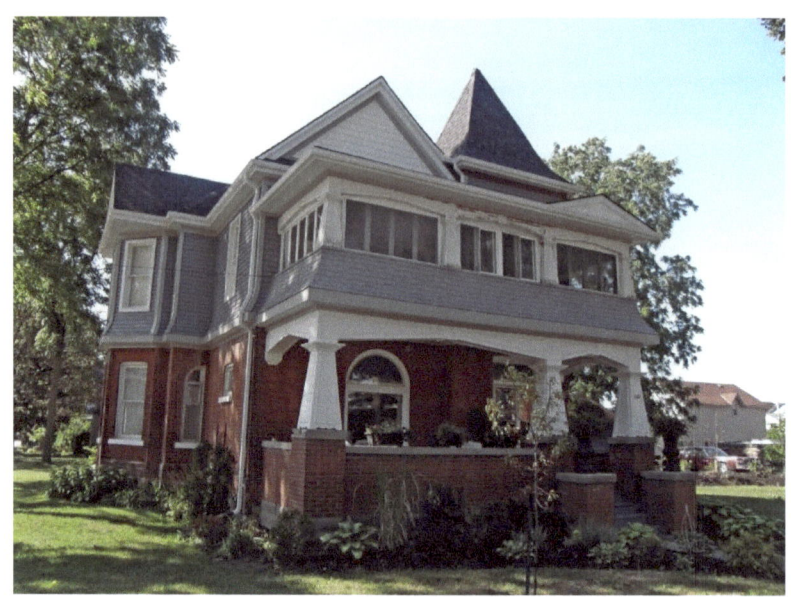

#100 - Queen Anne style – turret

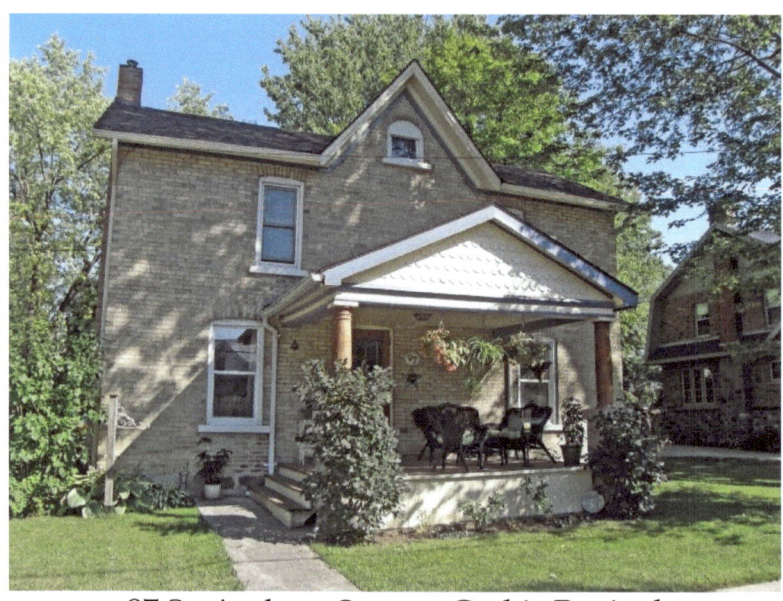

97 St. Andrew Street – Gothic Revival

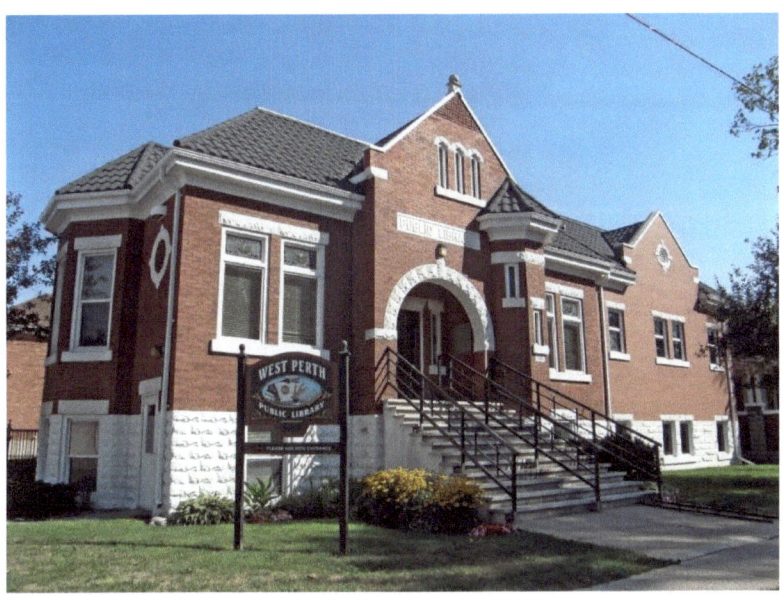

The West Perth Public Library began as the Mitchell Mechanics' Institute which was established in 1854 to provide area members with access to various technical and scientific materials. The building is a single storey with exposed basement and has a centrally located main entrance accessed by a series of steps meant to symbolize man's rise to higher levels through reading. The library possesses beautiful stained glass windows many of which incorporate the 'torch of learning' design. The row of smaller windows on the east wall that are situated high on the wall was to allow for rows of bookshelves along the wall.

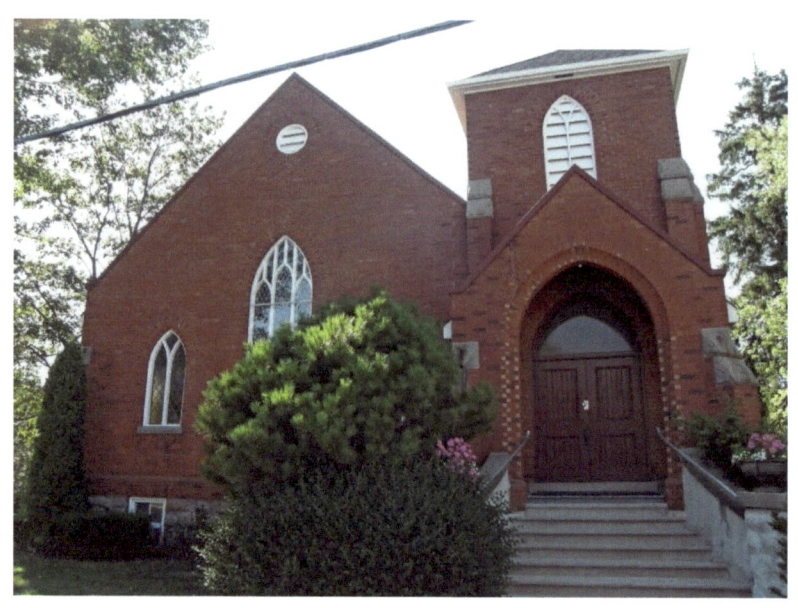

Trinity Anglican Church - 1858

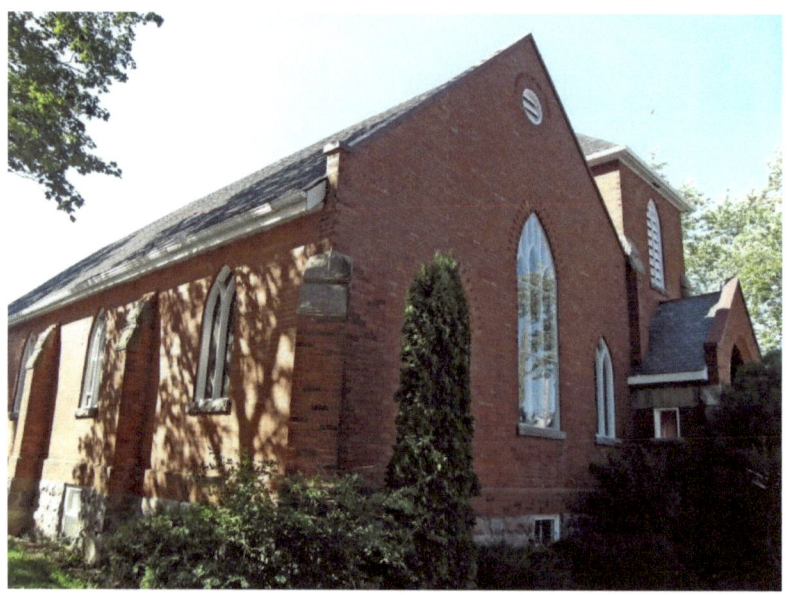

Gothic

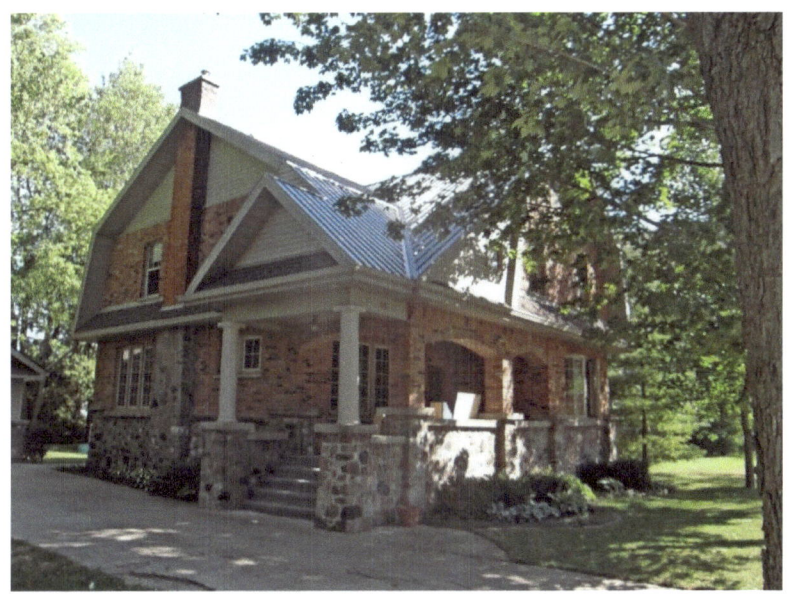

95 St. Andrew Street

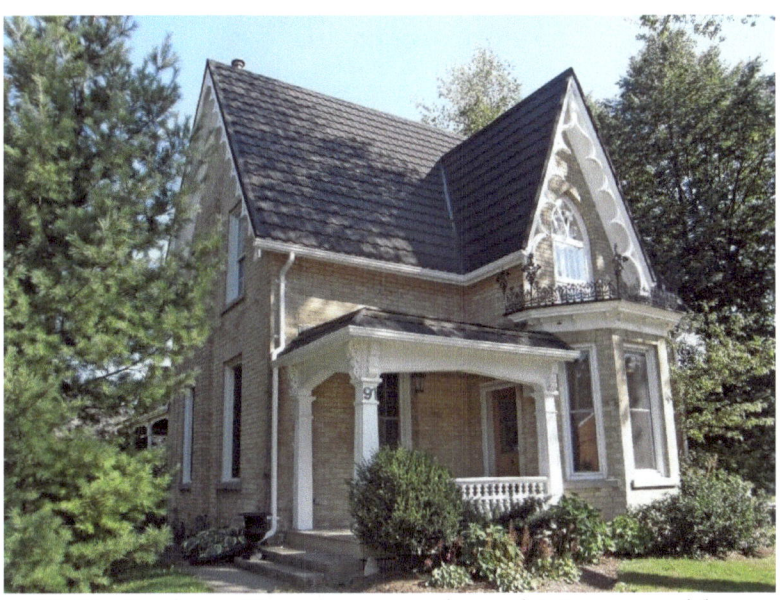

91 St. Andrew Street – verge board trim on gables,
iron cresting above bay window

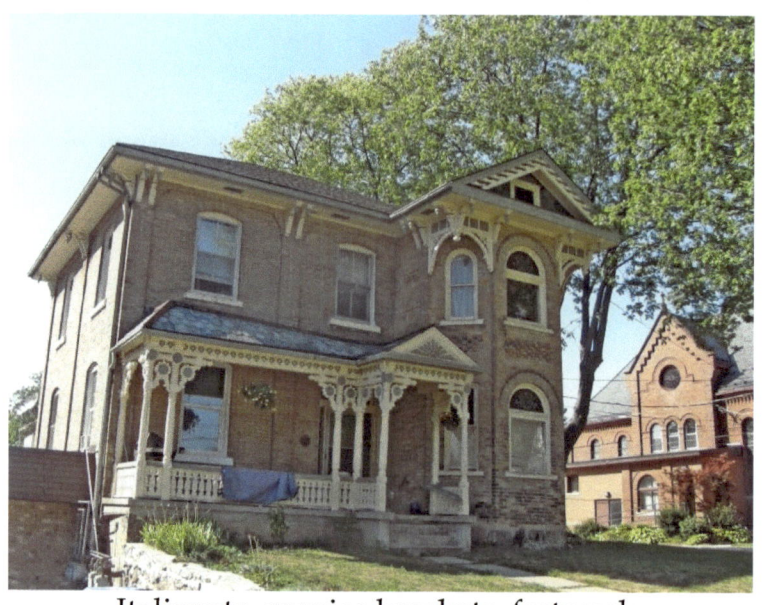

Italianate, cornice brackets, fretwork,
decorative pillars on porch and pediment,
2½ storey tower-like bay

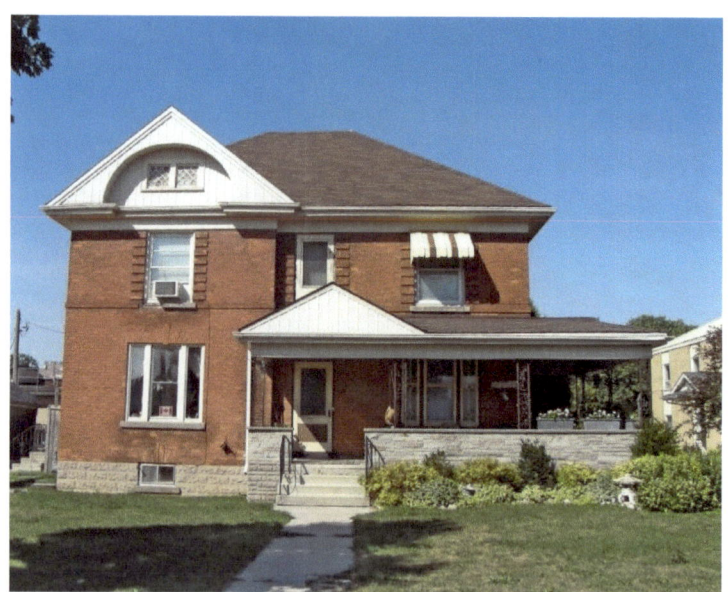

Edwardian

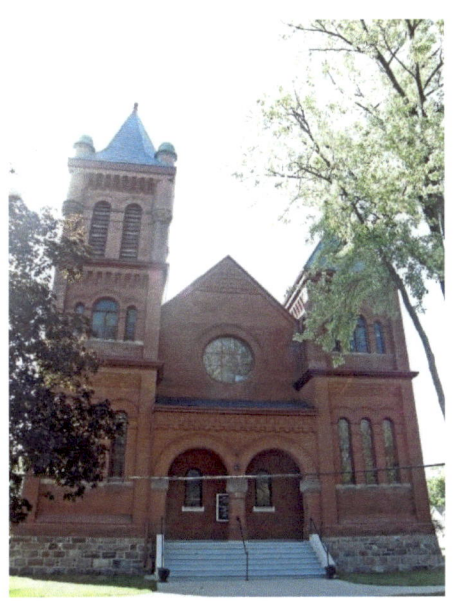

92 Main Street - Knox Presbyterian Church, Romanesque style
window voussoirs, bevelled dentil moulding

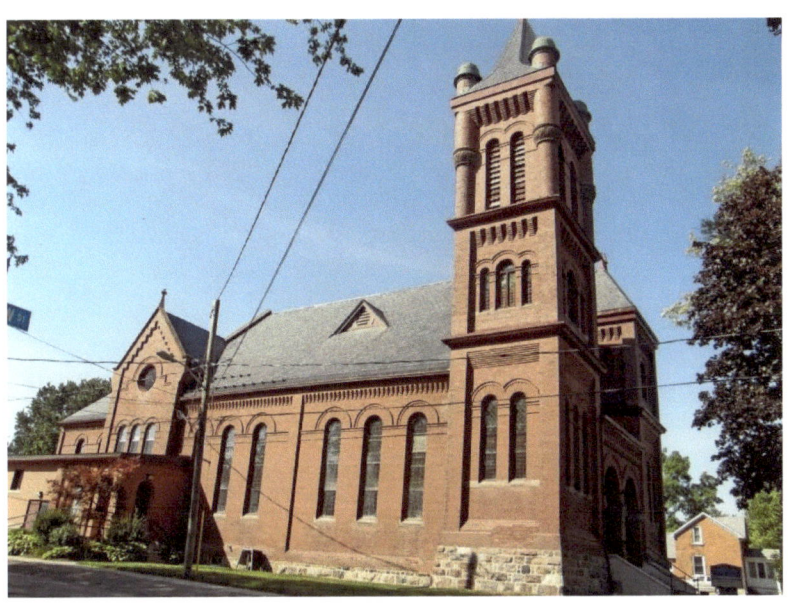

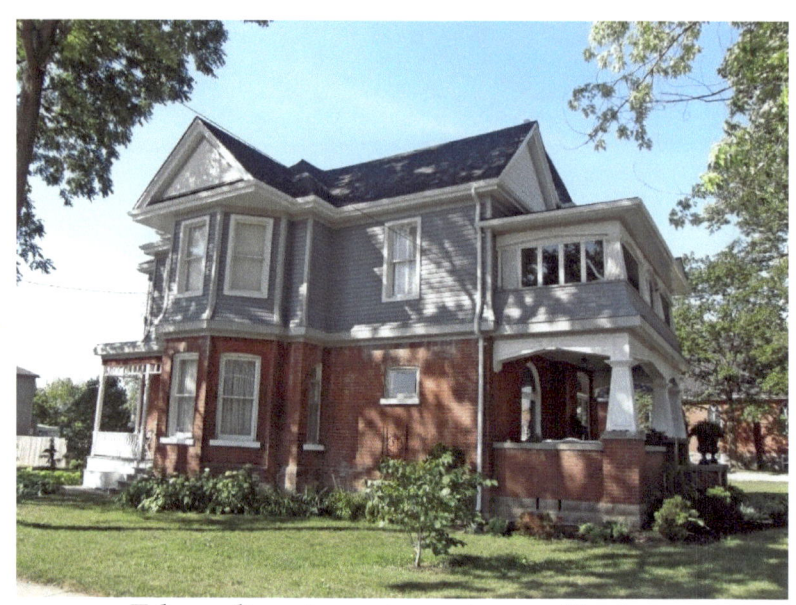

Edwardian, two-storey tower-like bay

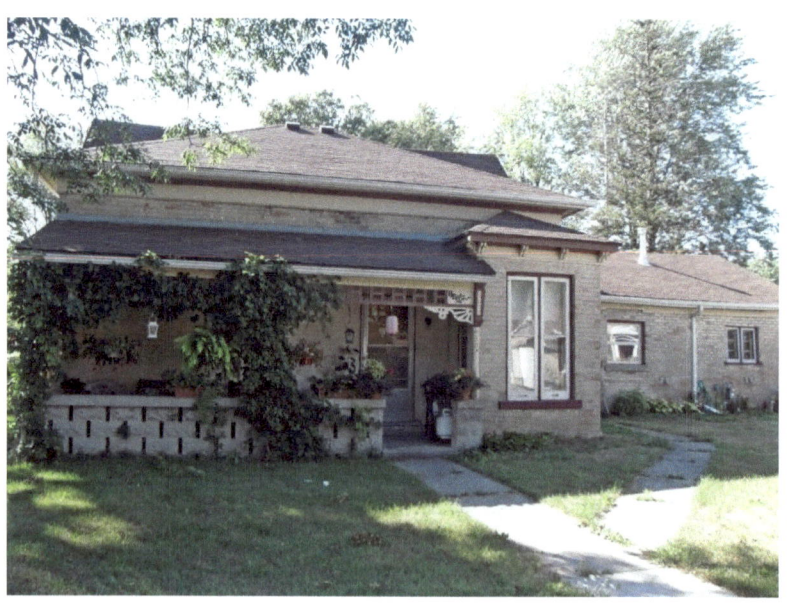

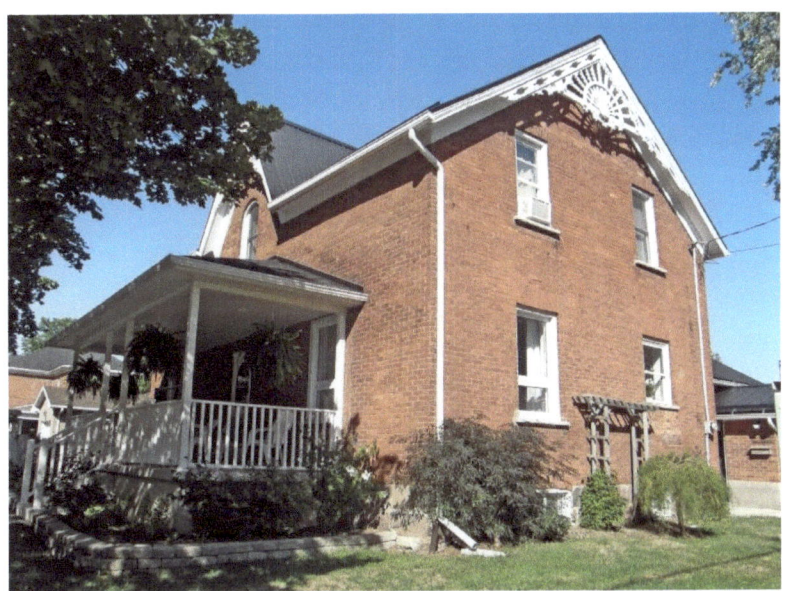

Gothic Revival, verge board trim on gable

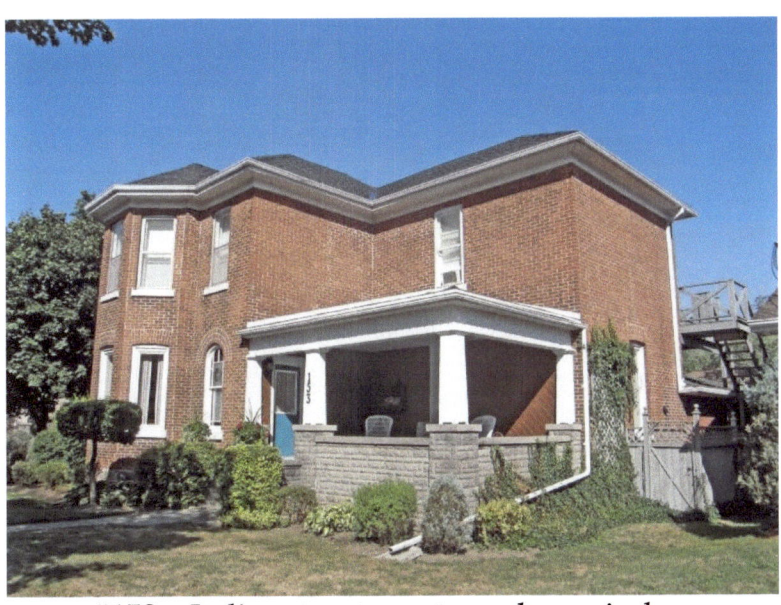

#153 – Italianate – two-storey bay window

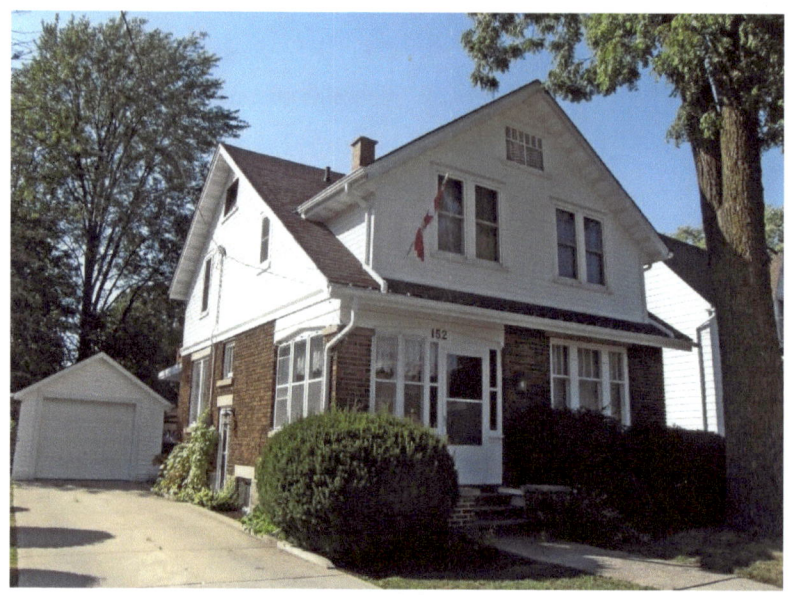

#152

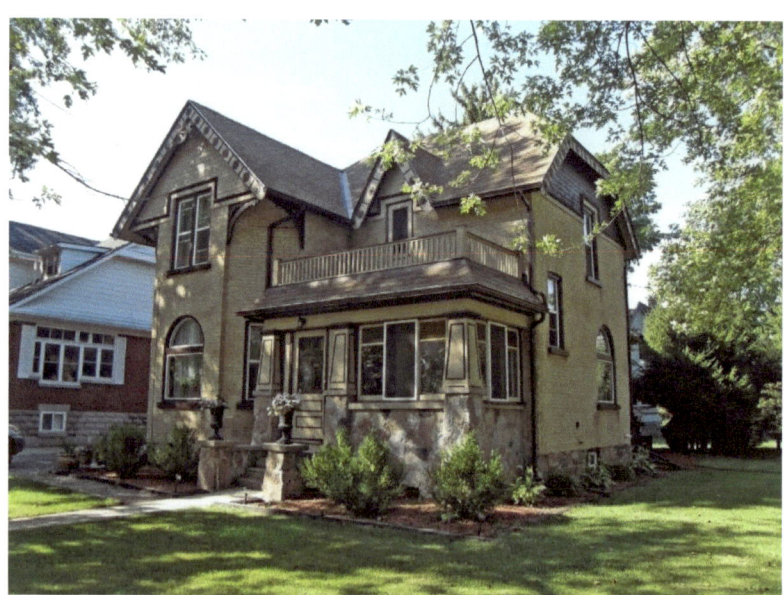

#91 - Gothic Revival – verge board trim on gables,
2nd floor balcony, fretwork, cobblestone basement

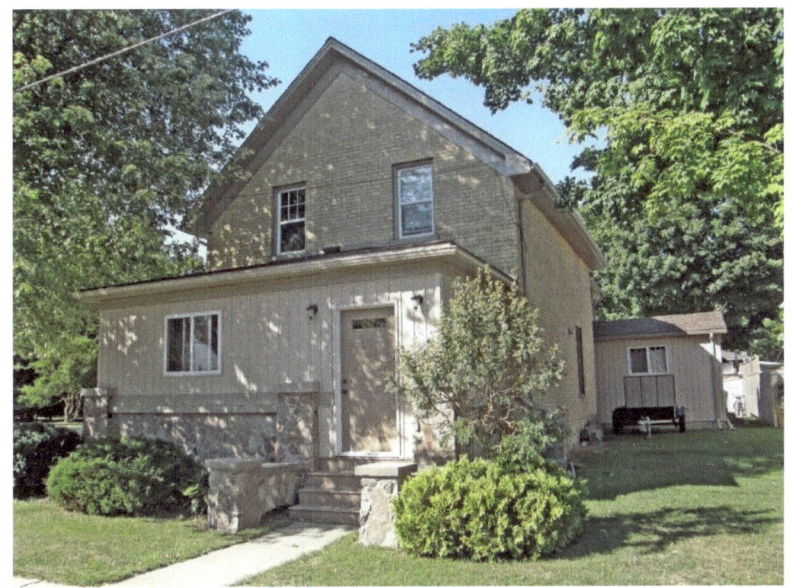

Waterloo Street - Gothic

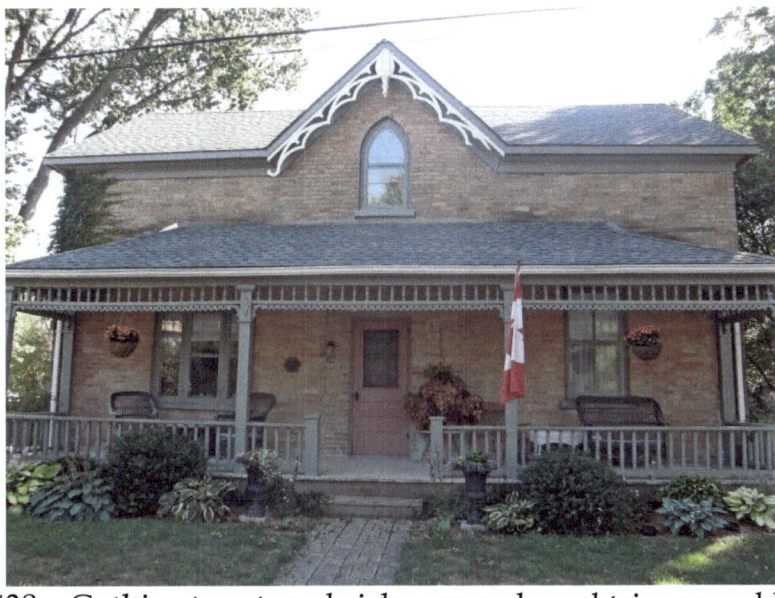

#38 – Gothic - two-tone bricks, verge board trim on gable

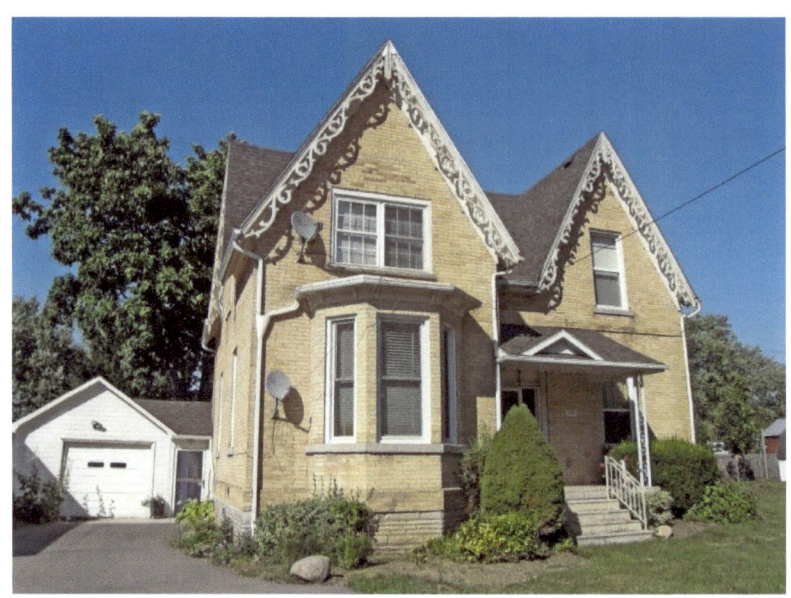

Waterloo Street – Gothic Revival, verge board trim on gables, bay window

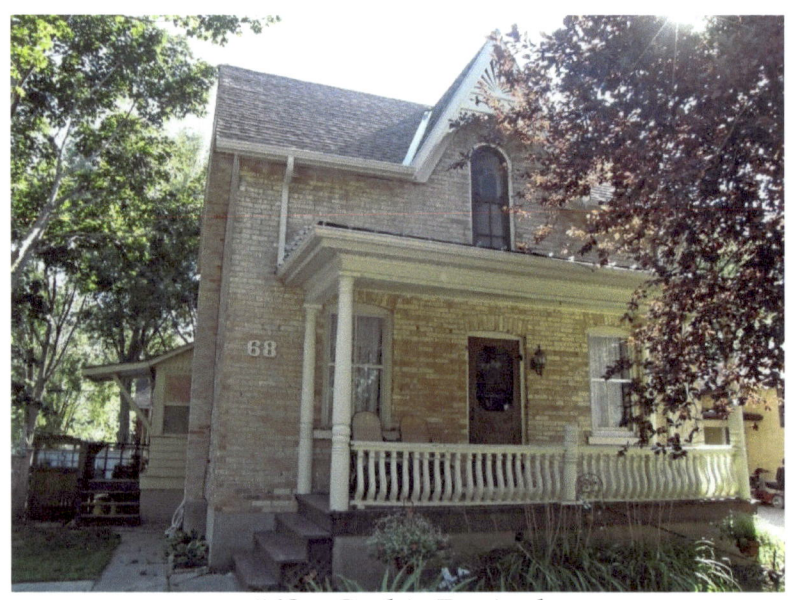

#68 – Gothic Revival

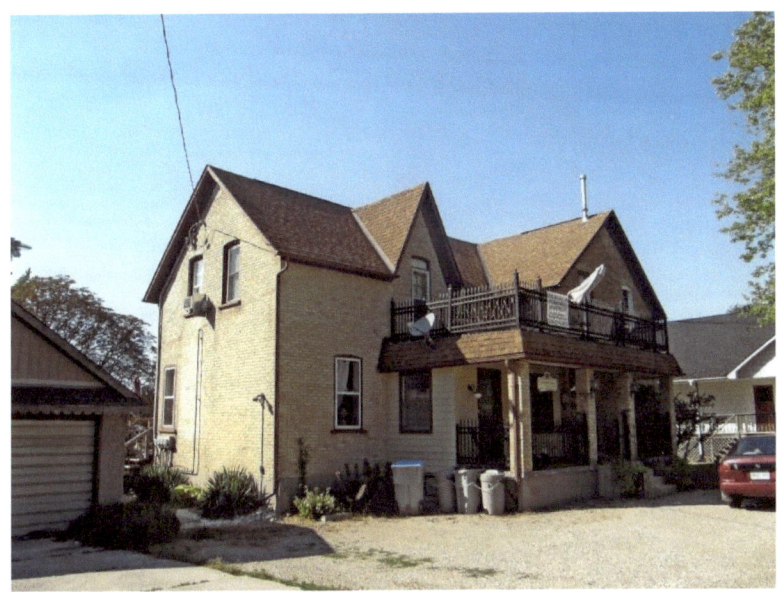

St. George Street – Gothic Revival, second floor balcony

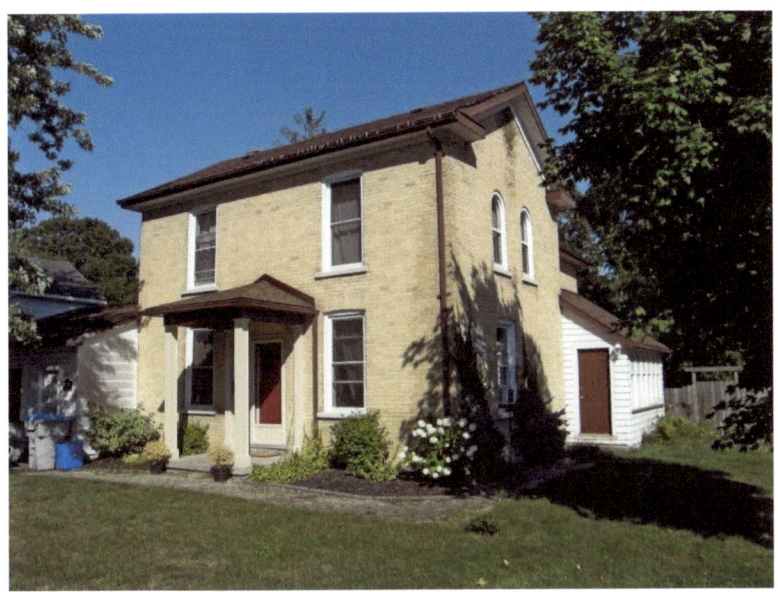

Cornice return on gable

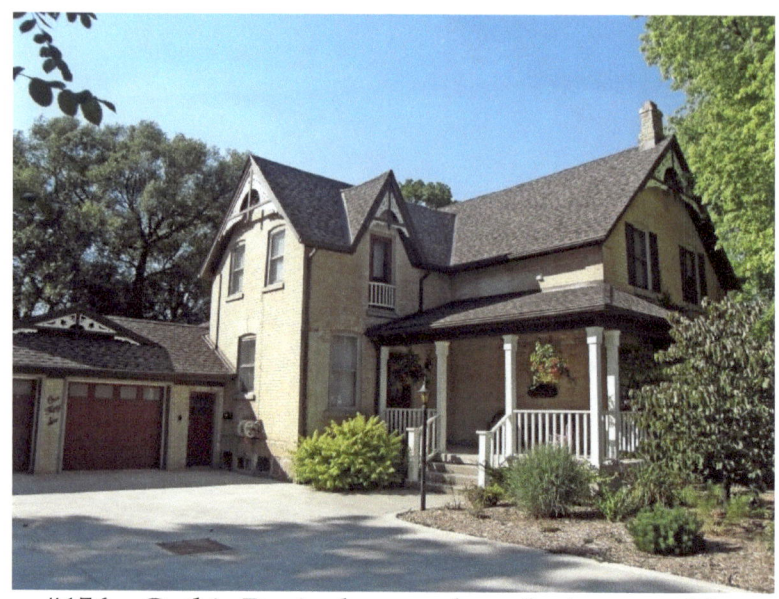

#156 – Gothic Revival, verge board trim on gables

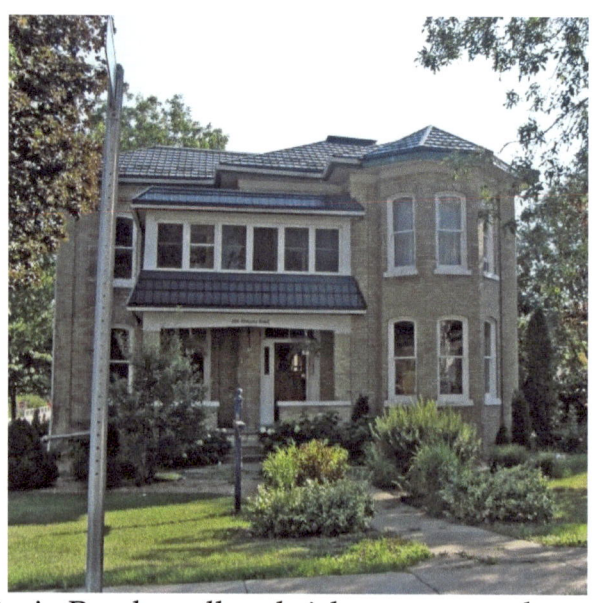

168 Ontario Road – yellow brick, two-storey bay window

Walton

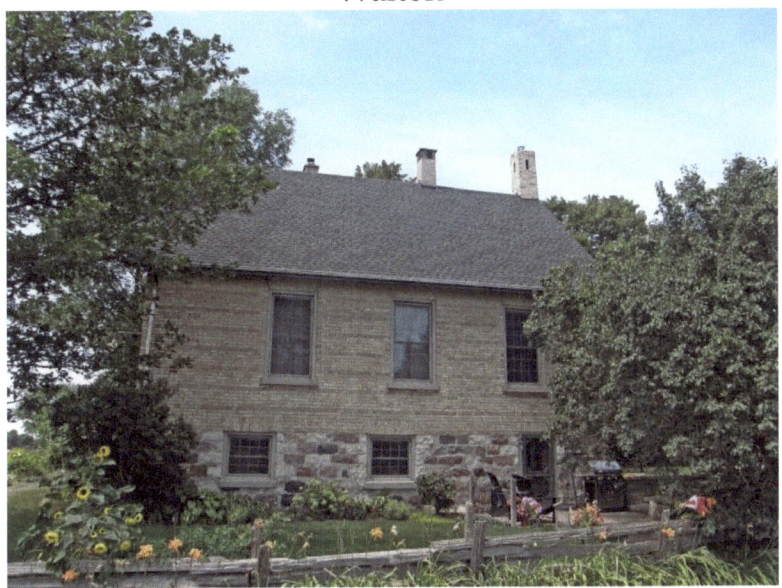

Cobblestone basement

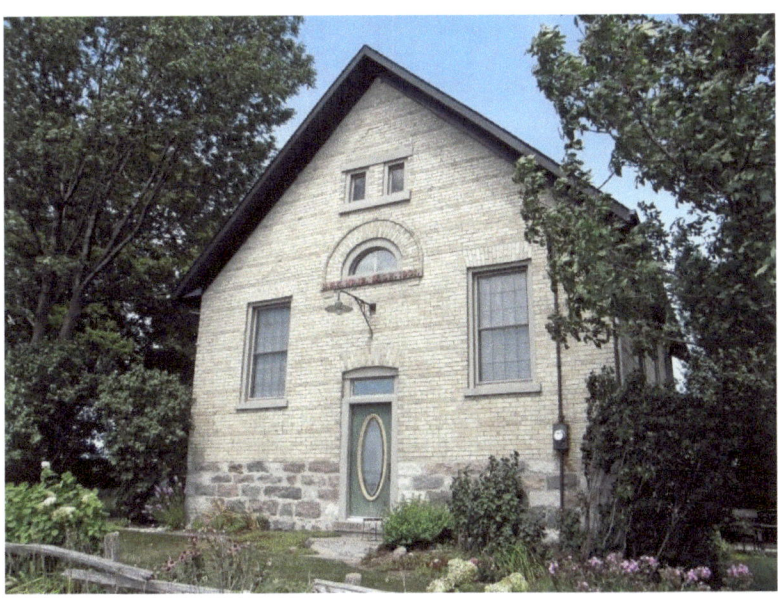

U.S.S. No. 12 M.S.H. – Gothic, cobblestone basement

Whitechurch

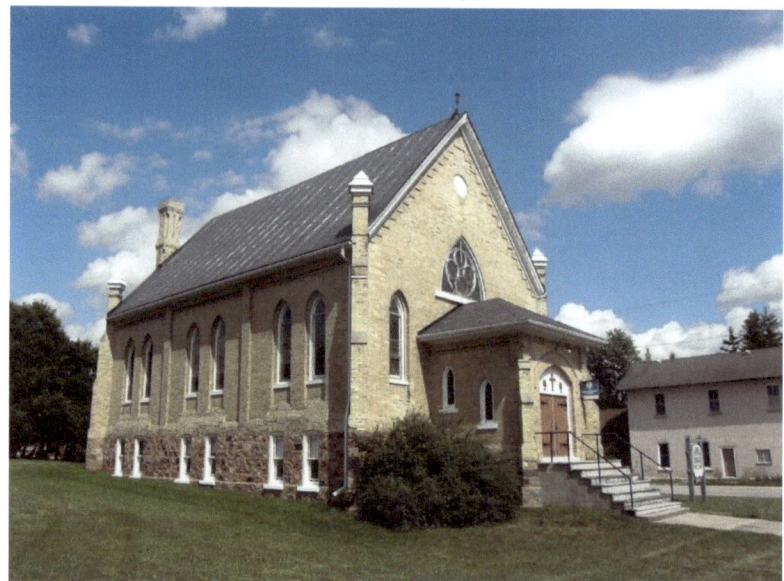

Chalmers Presbyterian Church – buttresses, rose window

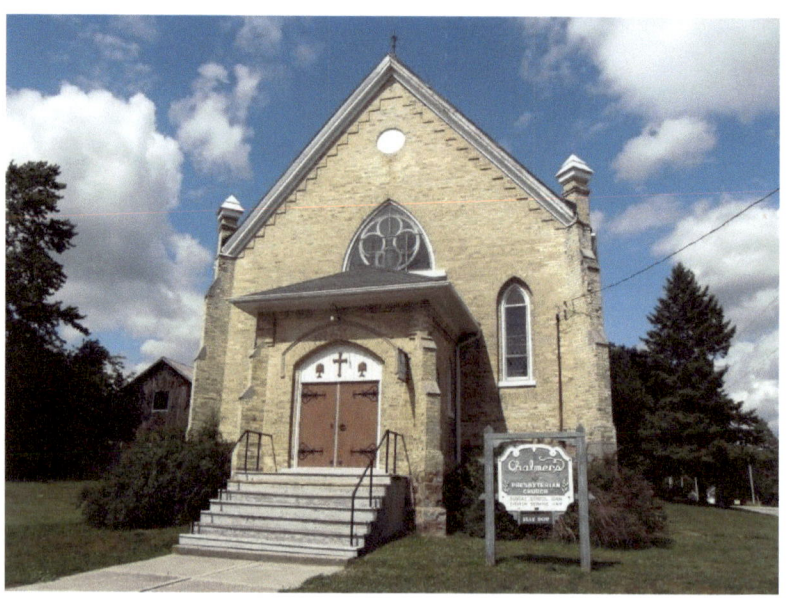

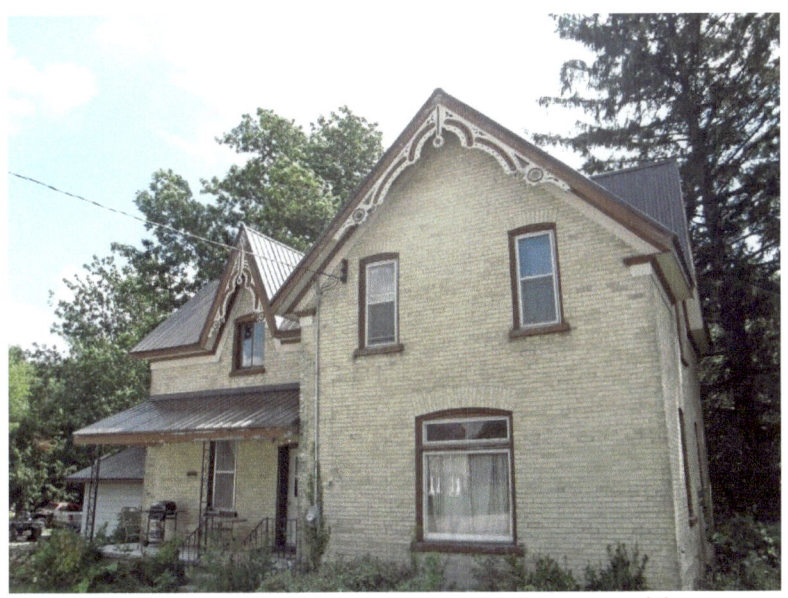

Gothic Revival, verge board trim on gables

Winthrop

Cavan United Church 1907 – Gothic – buttresses, bevelled
dentil moulding, lancet windows

Architectural Terms

Bay Window: A window that projects out from a wall, in a semicircular, rectangular, or polygonal design. Used frequently in Gothic and Victorian designs. Example: Waterloo Street, Mitchell, Page 48	
Brackets: a decorative or weight-bearing structural element which forms a right angle with one side against a wall and the other under a projecting surface such as an eave or roof. Example: Mitchell, Page 42	
Buttress: a masonry structure built against or projecting from a wall which serves to support or reinforce the wall. In Canadian architecture, they are sometimes used for decoration. Example: Page 18	
Cobblestone architecture: Refers to the use of cobblestones embedded in mortar as a method for erecting walls on houses and commercial buildings. Example: Page 9, 10	
Cornice: originally the wooden overhang of the roof. With the use of stone, brick, iron and steel, the cornice is any projecting shelf at the top of a ceiling or roof. They can be very decorative.	

Cornice Return: decorative element on the end of a gable. Example: Mitchell, Page 49	
Cupola: A domed or curved roof rising from a building as a decorative element. Example: Page 11	
Dentil Moulding: an even series of rectangles used as ornamental decoration in cornices. Example:	
Dichromatic brickwork: the use of two colours of brick, tile or slate to decorate a façade. Example: Lucknow Presbyterian Church, Page 21	
Dormer: (French for "sleep") a gable end window that pierces through the plane of a sloping roof surface to create usable space in the top floor or attic of a building by adding headroom. Example: Auburn	
Fretwork: interlaced decorative design resembling a bracket Example: Mitchell, Page 42	

Gable: the triangular portion of a wall between the edges of a sloping roof. Example: Dublin, see Page 29	
Hipped Roof: a roof where all sides slope downwards to the walls with no gables. Example: Campbell Street, see Page 14	
Iron Cresting: A decorative ornament along the top of a roof. Iron cresting was popular in the Baroque era and also in Italianate, Victorian, Second Empire and Queen Anne styles of architecture. Example: 91 St. Andrew Street, Mitchell, see Page 41	
Keystones and Voussoirs: a voussoir is a wedge-shaped element used in building an arch. A keystone is the central stone that locks all the stones into position, allowing the arch to bear weight. A keystone is often enlarged and embellished. Example: Dublin, see Page 28	
Lancet Window: a tall, narrow window with a pointed arch at its top. Example: Auburn, see Page 23	
Mansard Roof: This style was popularized by Francois Mansart (1598-1666), an accomplished architect of the French Baroque period and especially fashionable during the Second French Empire (1852-1870). This roof is almost flat on the top section, with two slopes on each of its sides with the lower slope at a steeper angle than the upper and having dormer windows. Example: Campbell Street, Lucknow	

Pediment: a triangular section above the horizontal structure (entablature), typically supported by columns. The inside of the triangle is called the tympanum. Example: 635 Outram Street, see Page 20	
Pilaster: a slightly projecting column built into or applied to the face of a wall for additional structural support. Example: see Page 15	
Quoin: masonry blocks at the corner of a wall, often a decorative feature, usually larger or of a different colour than the rest of the wall. Example: 638 Outram Street, Lucknow, Page 20	
Rose Window: a circular window with ornamental tracery radiating from the centre. Example: Auburn, see Page 23	
Turret: a small tower that projects from the wall of a building. Example:	
Verge board and Finial: also called bargeboards – hang from the projecting end of a roof and are often elaborately carved and ornamented. **Finial:** ornament added to the top of a gable, pinnacle, canopy or spire – a Gothic element.	
Window Hood: the piece above window openings, usually of an ornate design, and covers the top third of the opening. Hoods are commonly placed above arched or curved openings on both windows and doors. Example: Mitchell, see Page 30	

Edwardian, 1900-1930 – This style bridges the ornate and elaborate styles of the Victorian era and the simplified styles of the 20th century. Balanced facades, simple roof lines, dormer windows, large front porches, and smooth brick surfaces are its characteristics. Example: Mitchell, see Page 42	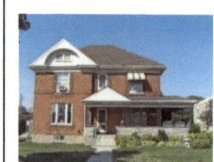
Gothic Revival, 1830-1890 – These decorative buildings have sharply-pitched gables with highly detailed verge boards, pointed-arch window openings, and dichromatic brickwork. It is a common style in Ontario. Example: Mitchell, see Page 48	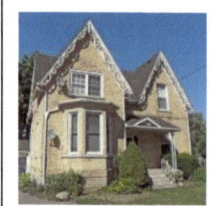
Italianate, 1850-1900 – It has wide-bracketed eaves, belvederes, wrap-around verandahs. Example: Auburn, see Page 24	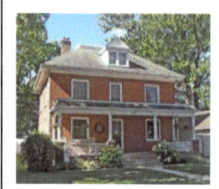
Queen Anne, 1885-1900 – This style is distinguished by an irregular outline featuring a combination of an offset tower, broad gables, projecting two-storey bays, verandahs, multi-sloped roofs, and tall, decorative chimneys. A mixture of brick and wood is common. Windows often have one large single-paned bottom sash and small panes in the upper sash. Example: Mitchell, see Page 38	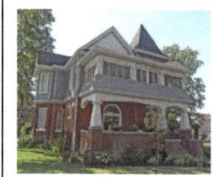

Romanesque Revival, 1880-1910 – This style hearkens back to medieval architecture of the 11th and 12th centuries with a heavy appearance, blocky towers and rounded arches. Example: Knox Presbyterian Church, Mitchell	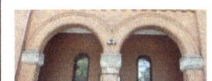
Second Empire, 1860-1880 – The mansard roof is the most noteworthy feature of this style and is evidence of the French origins. Projecting central towers and one or two-storey bays can also be present. Example: Campbell Street, Lucknow	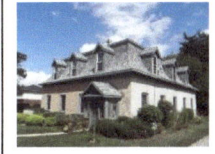